Level 1

MUSICIANSHIP FOR THE OLDER BEGINNER

by James Bastien

The Bastien Older Beginner Piano Library

PREFACE

MUSICIANSHIP FOR THE OLDER BEGINNER is designed to be used as a companion book to **THE OLDER BEGINNER PIANO COURSE.** Theory, Technic, and Sight Reading materials are correlated unit by unit to the basic course. It may also be used with any other piano course.

The **Theory** portion contains a combination of written exercises and keyboard harmony.

The **Technic** portion is designed to develop hand and finger coordination and facility, and to develop ease and control at the keyboard. Dynamics and tempo are to be suggested by the teacher. Transposition is indicated for some exercises; additional transposition may be suggested at the teachers' discretion.

The **Sight Reading** portion provides additional reading to reinforce new concepts. A variety of reading experiences is provided to relieve monotony. The student should give a brief pre-study analysis before playing: 1) tap or clap the rhythm; 2) observe the clef, key and time signature. While playing he should 1) keep his eyes on the music; 2) look ahead; 3)keep going. Transposition may be assigned at the teacher's discretion.

This balanced program will provide the student with a thorough beginning music program in basic fundamentals.

Suggested Use of Materials with **THE OLDER BEGINNER PIANO COURSE, LEVEL 1**

When the student reaches **page 5,** he is ready to begin .... **Musicianship, Level 1** (WP34)
When the student reaches **page 14,** he is ready to begin .... **Music Flashcards** (GP27)
When the student reaches **page 15,** he is ready to begin .... **Notespeller, Level 1** (WP20)
When the student reaches **page 44,** he is ready to begin .... **Classic Themes by the Masters** (WP40)
When the student reaches **page 46,** he is ready to begin .... **Religious Favorites** (WP41)
When the student reaches **page 48,** he is ready to begin .... **Favorite Melodies the World Over, Level 1** (WP37)
When the student reaches **page 53,** he is ready to begin .... **Pop, Rock 'N Blues, Book 1** (GP37)

Published by Kjos West.
Distributed by Neil A. Kjos Music Company.
National Order Desk, 4382 Jutland Dr., San Diego, CA 92117

ISBN 0-8497-5031-8
Cover Photo: Harry Crosby/Photophile

CONTENTS

UNIT 1
THEORY

WHITE KEY NAMES

1. Write the names of these white keys.

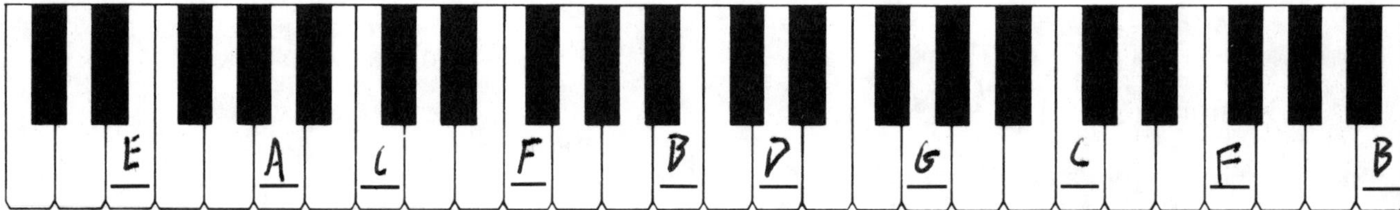

C MAJOR FIVE FINGER POSITION

2. Write the C Major Five Finger Position forward on this keyboard. Play this position on the piano in different places. Use either hand. Say the letters aloud as you play.

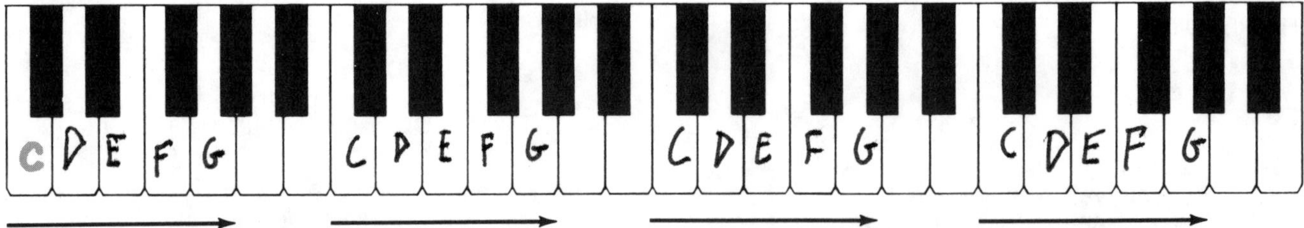

3. Write the C Major Five Finger Position backward on this keyboard. Play this position on the piano in different places. Use either hand. Say the letters aloud as you play.

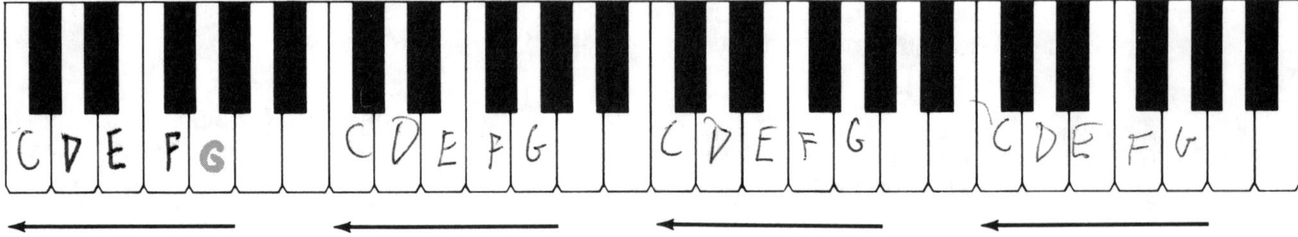

INTERVALS (2nds, 3rds)

The distance between two tones is called an INTERVAL. On the keyboard, neighbor white keys are a 2nd apart. Skipped white keys are a 3rd apart.

Examples of White Key Intervals

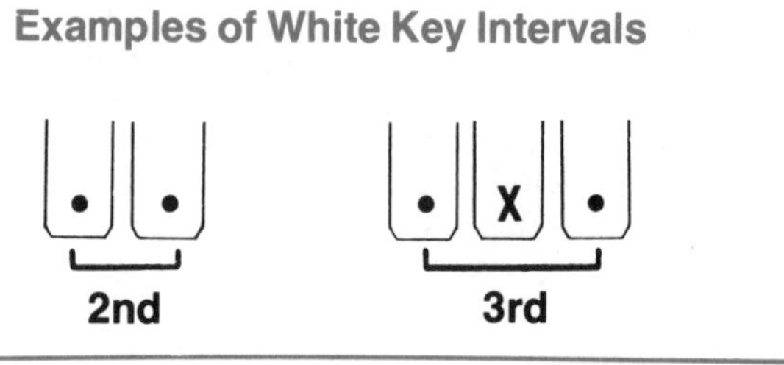

4. Play some intervals of 2nds and 3rds on the piano. Use either hand.

5. Write intervals of 2nds up or down from the given letters. Play these intervals on the piano. Use either hand.

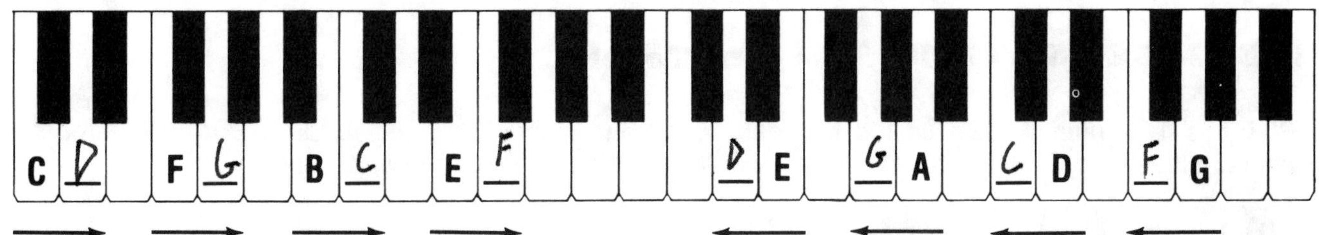

6. Write intervals of 3rds up or down from the given letters. Play these intervals on the piano. Use either hand.

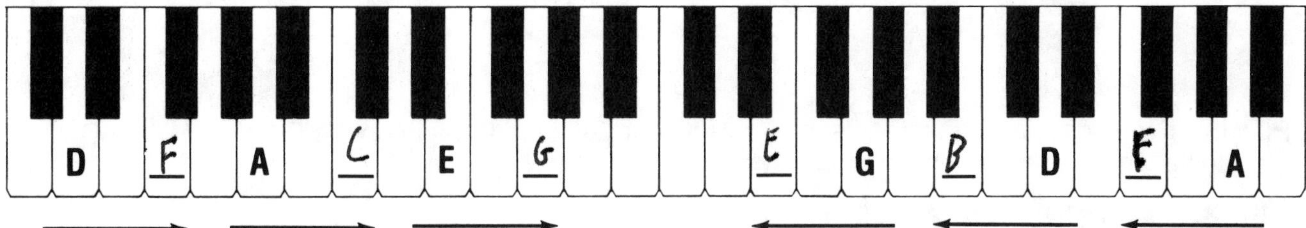

RHYTHM

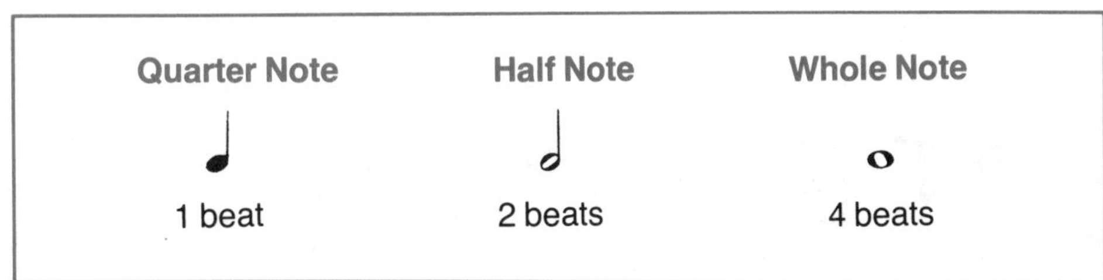

7. Clap and count this rhythm pattern.

8. Tap this rhythm pattern with both hands. Count aloud while tapping. The notes above the line are for your Right Hand; the notes below the line are for your Left Hand.

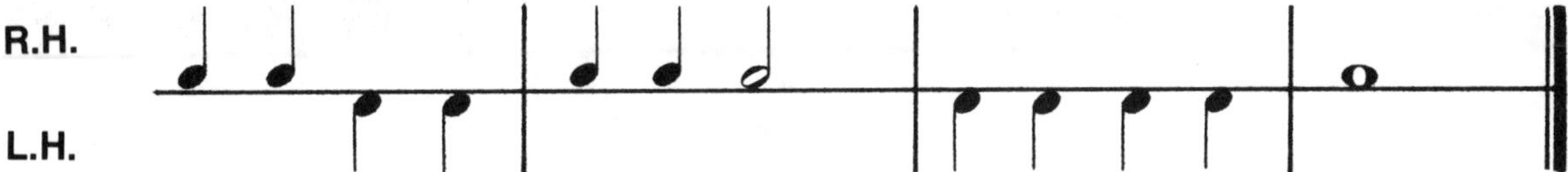

THE C CHORD

The C chord is formed from three of the keys in the C Major Five Finger Position. The keys within the chord are a 3rd apart.	G E C **The lowest letter gives the chord its name.**

9. Play C chords in the rhythm given in Number 7 above. Play with your Left Hand. Count aloud as you play.

TECHNIC

FIVE-FINGER PATTERNS (Legato Touch)

1. Play this five-finger pattern up the keyboard with your Right Hand. Use a LEGATO touch (smooth, connected). Begin on Middle C, then D, E, etc., continuing the pattern up the white keys.

2. Play this five-finger pattern up the keyboard with your Left Hand. Begin on the C below Middle C, then D, E, etc., continuing the pattern up the white keys.

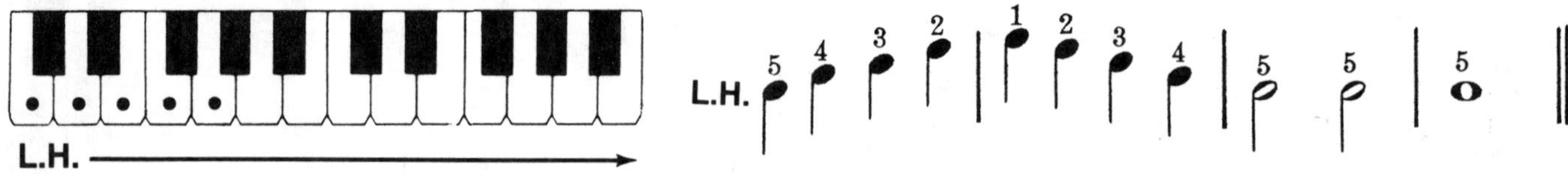

3. Play this pattern up the keyboard with your Right Hand. Begin on Middle C, then D, E, etc., continuing the pattern up the white keys.

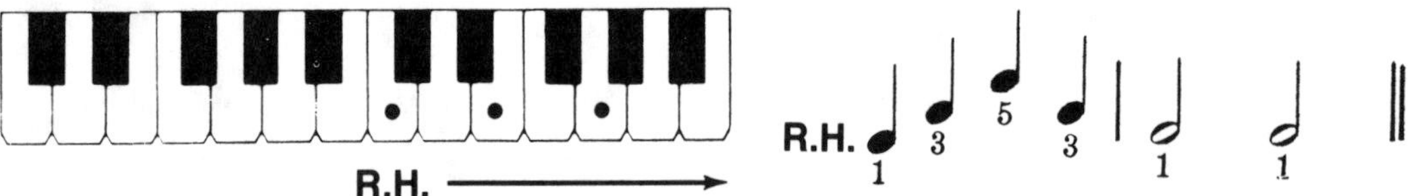

4. Play this pattern up the keyboard with your Left Hand. Begin on the C below Middle C, then D, E, etc., continuing the pattern up the white keys.

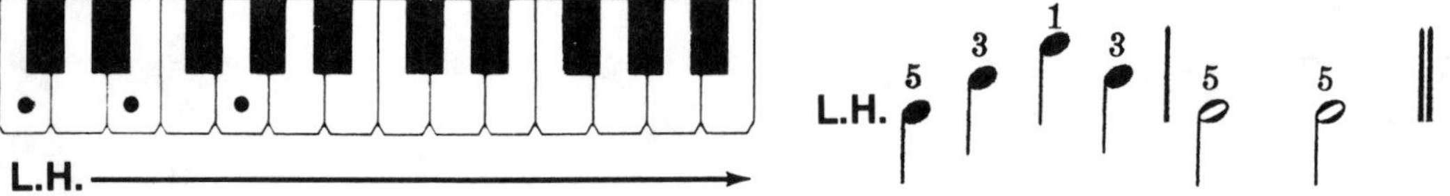

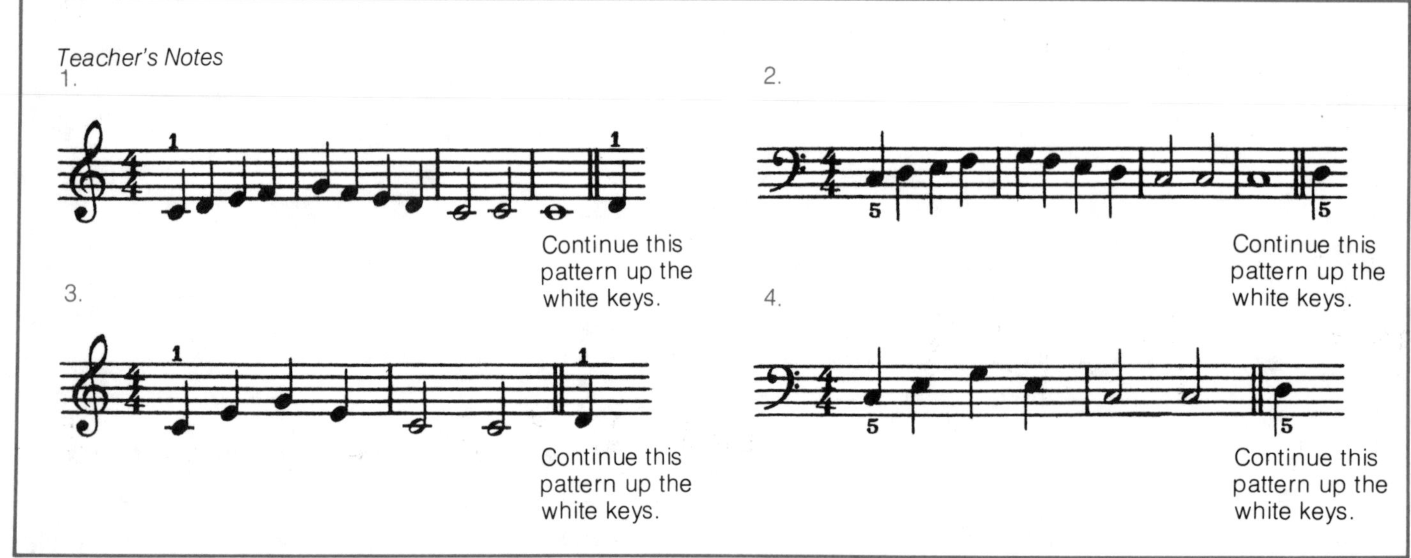

SIGHT READING

PRACTICE DIRECTIONS

1. Clap and count the rhythm aloud before playing.
2. Find the position for both hands.
3. Watch the music while playing.
4. Play and sing the finger numbers aloud.
5. Play again and count the rhythm aloud.
6. Play again and sing the letter names of the notes aloud.

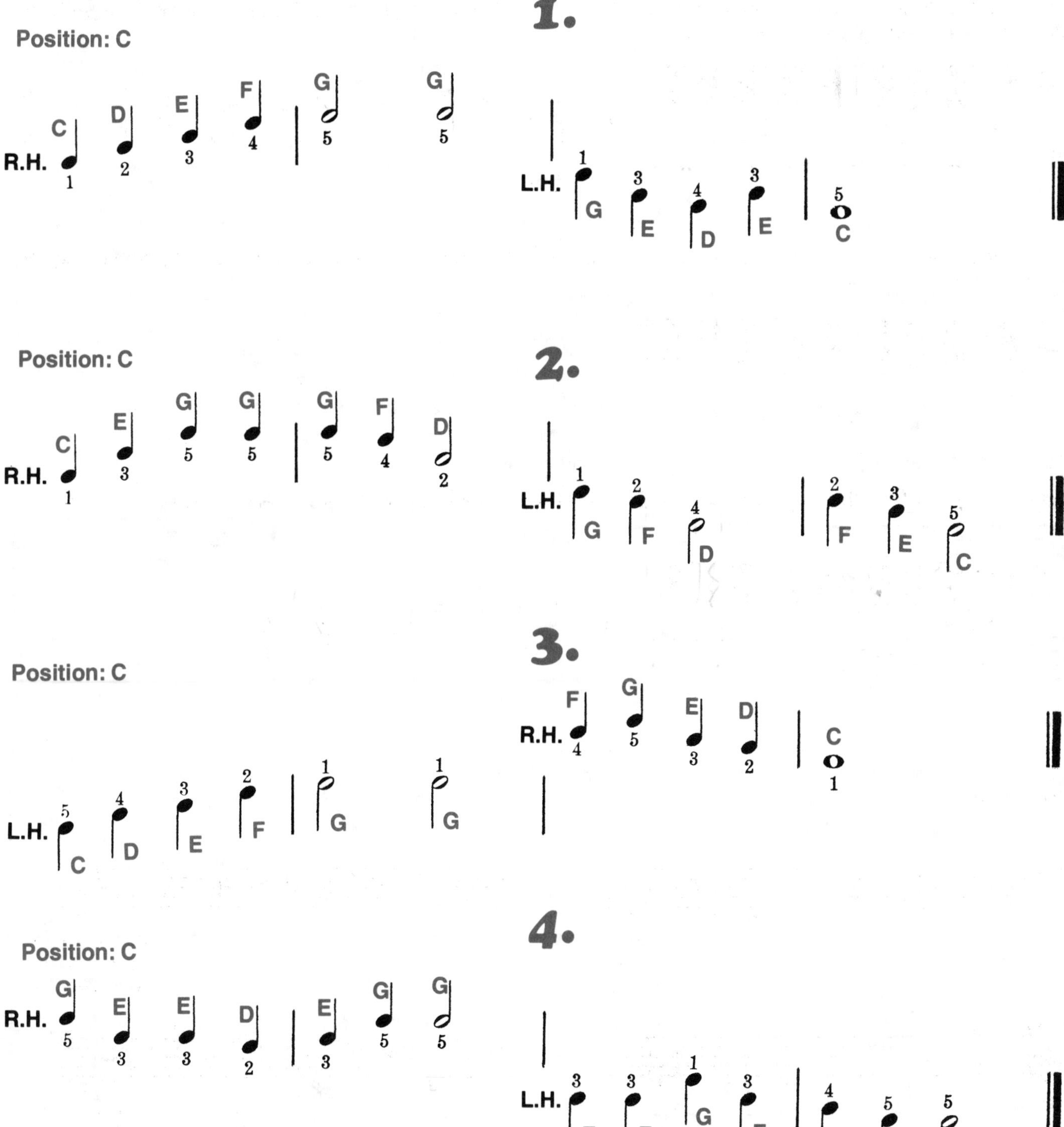

UNIT 2
THEORY

THE GRAND STAFF

Piano music is written on a GRAND STAFF which has two complete sets of lines and spaces. The upper part of the Grand Staff is called the Treble Staff. A Treble Clef or G clef 𝄞 is used at the beginning of this staff. The lower part of the Grand Staff is called the Bass Staff. A Bass Clef or F Clef sign 𝄢 is used at the beginning of this staff.

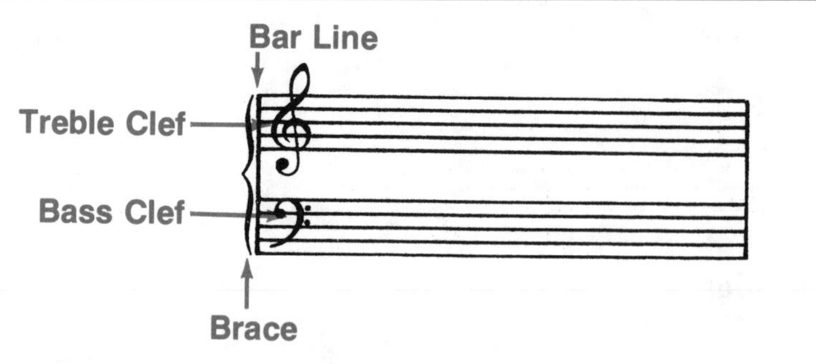

1. Draw some Treble Clef and Bass Clef signs on this Grand Staff.

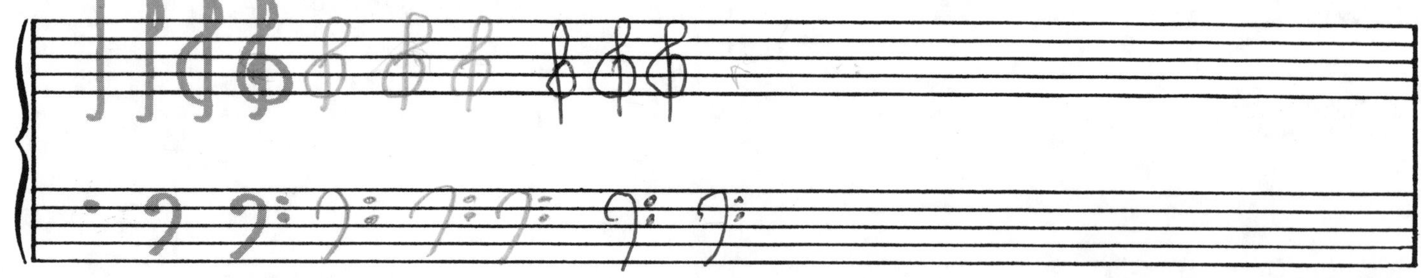

The Grand Staff is formed by joining together the Treble and Bass Staffs with a Brace and a Bar Line.

2. Make Grand Staffs by adding clef signs, braces and bar lines.

NOTES AND RESTS

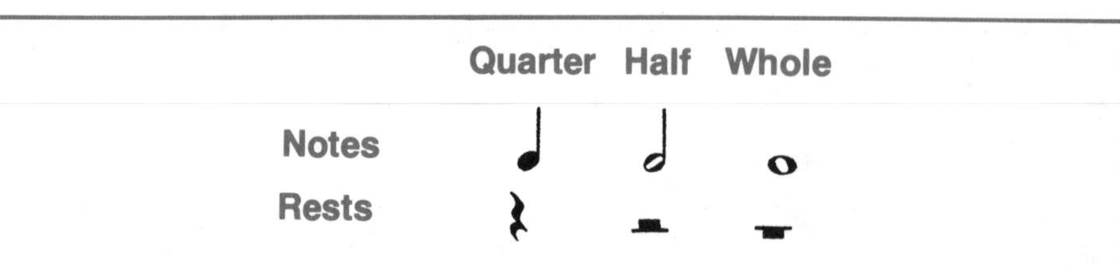

3. Draw each note and rest four times.

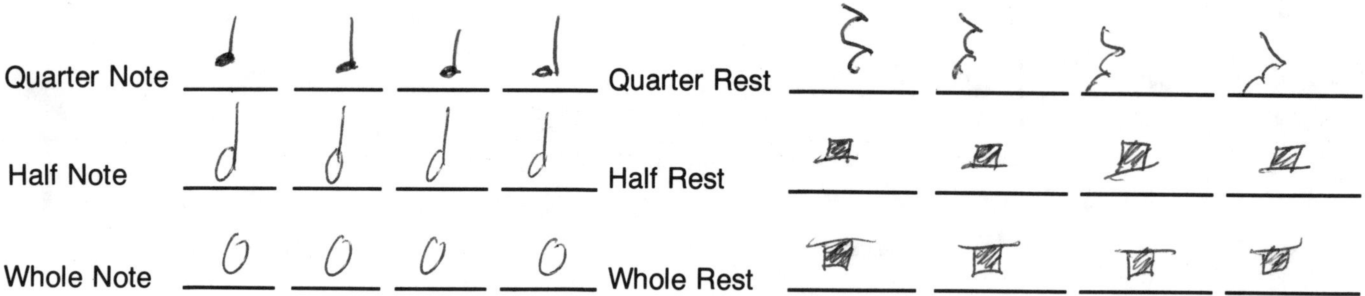

STEMMING NOTES

With the exception of the whole note, all notes have stems. Notes on or above the middle line of the staff have down stems; these stems are on the LEFT side of the notes. Notes below the middle line have up stems; these stems are on the RIGHT side of the notes.

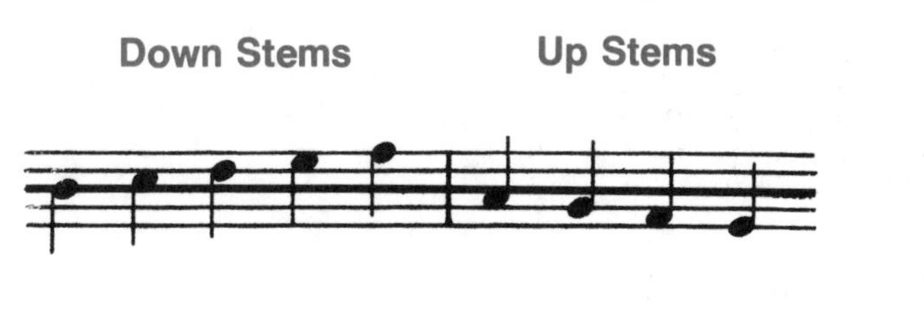

4. Draw stems on these note heads. Write the name of each note below it.

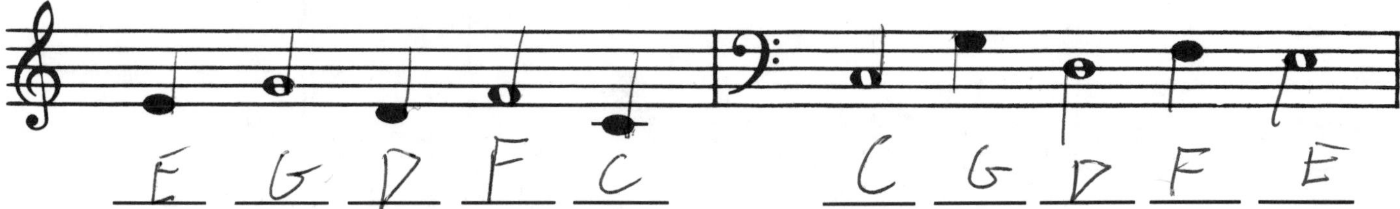

INTERVALS (through the 5th)

The distance in pitch between two notes is an INTERVAL. Note the similarity between 2nds and 4ths (line-space or space-line), and between 3rds and 5ths (line-line or space-space).

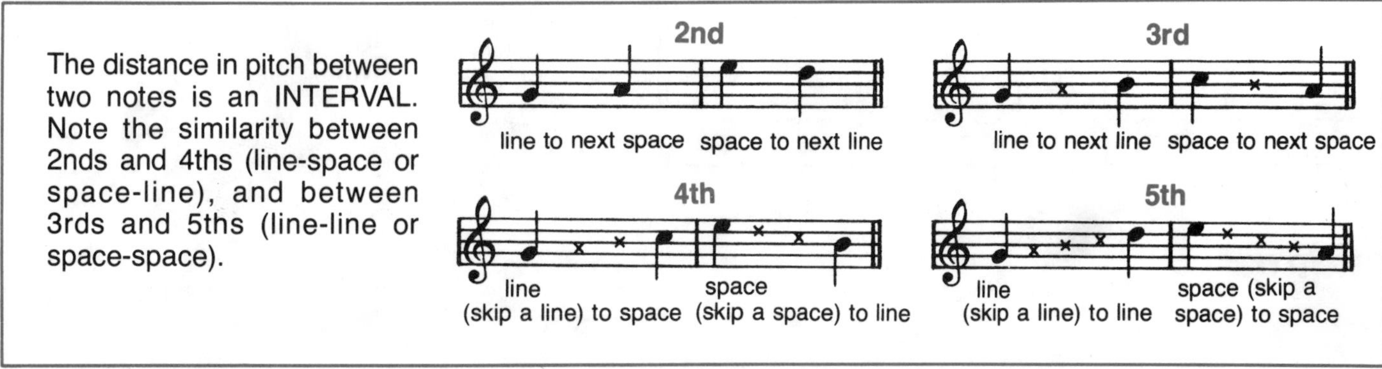

5. Name these intervals.

6. Draw notes up or down from the given notes to form these intervals. Write the letter names of both notes on the blanks below. Play these intervals.

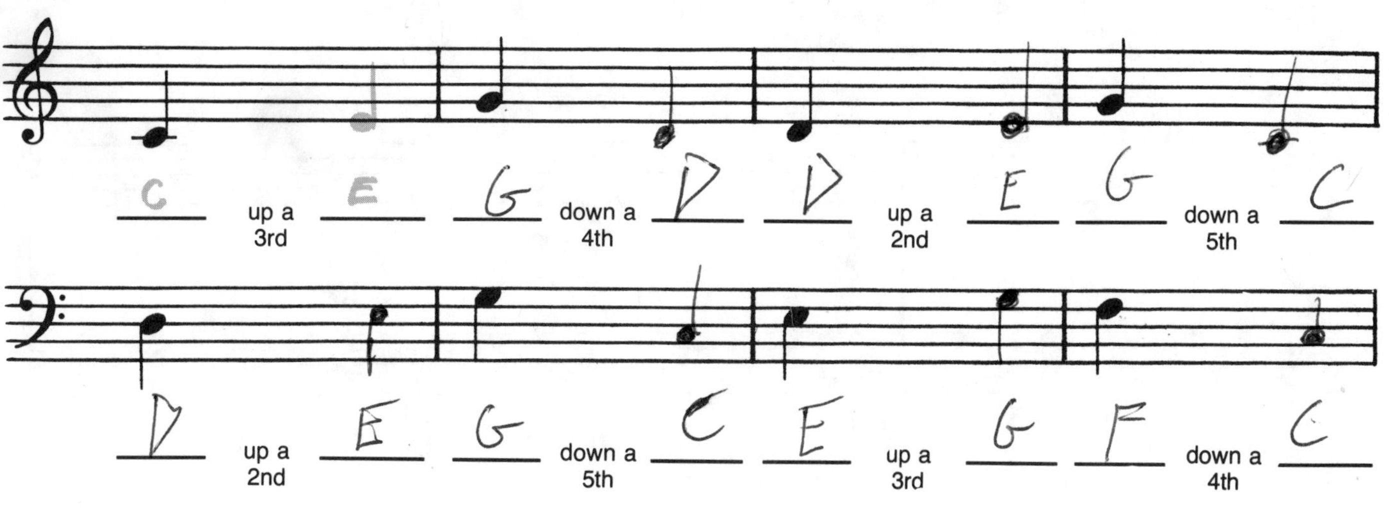

TECHNIC

FIVE-FINGER PATTERNS

Play hands separately at first. Use a legato touch.

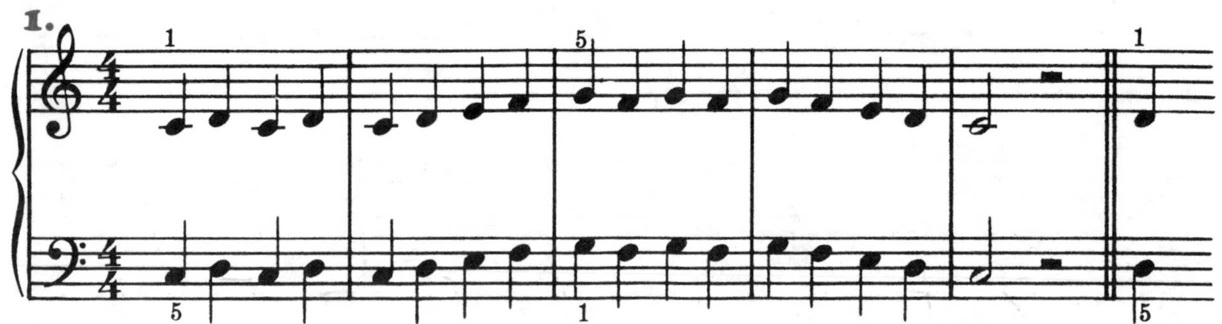

Continue this pattern up the white keys.

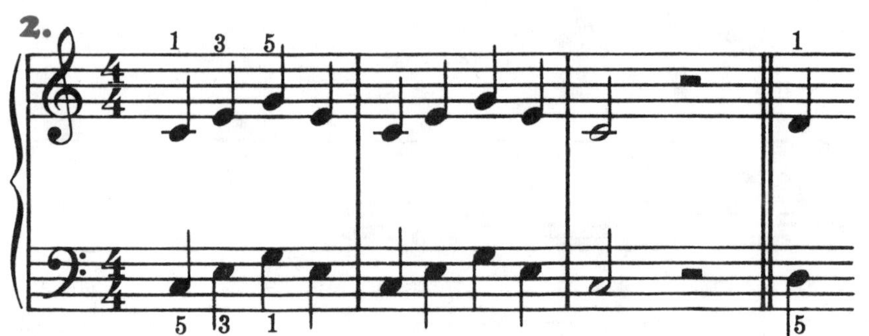

Continue this pattern up the white keys.

CHORDS

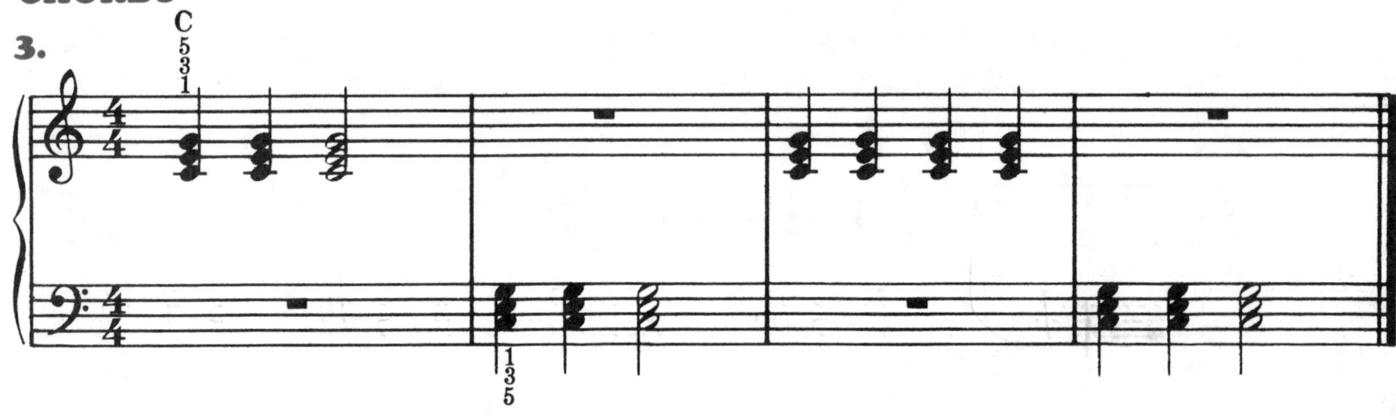

Play by "feel." Do not look down at your hands for the chord changes.

SIGHT READING

PRACTICE DIRECTIONS

1. Clap (or tap) and count the rhythm aloud before playing.
2. Find the position for both hands.
3. Watch the music while playing.
4. Play and count the rhythm aloud.
5. (optional) Play again and sing the letter names of the notes aloud.

UNIT 3
THEORY

EIGHTH NOTES

An EIGHTH NOTE receives HALF a beat in a time signature where a quarter note receives one beat. One eighth note has a FLAG (♪).

TWO EIGHTH NOTES equal one quarter note and receive a total of one beat. Two eighth notes are paired together with a BEAM (┌┐).

Eighth Note

♪ = 1/2 beat

Eighth Rest

𝄾 = 1/2 beat

Two Eighth Notes

♫ = ♩ (1 beat)

1. Draw the indicated single eighth notes on this staff. Play these notes.

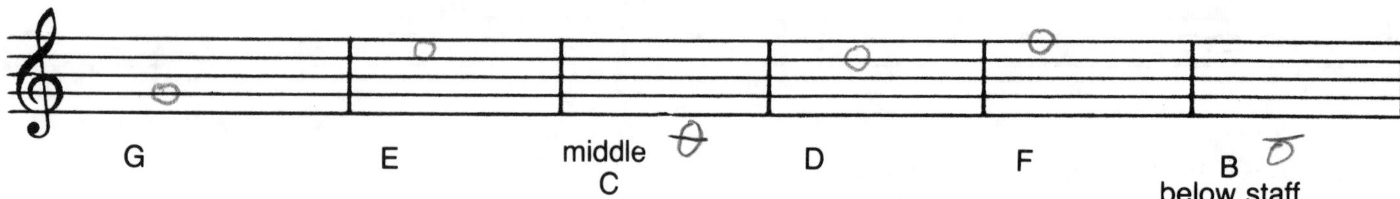

2. Draw the indicated eighth note pairs on this staff. Play these notes.

Eighth note pairs may be counted with numbers or by saying the note names in rhythm.

Count:	1	and	2	and	(etc.)
or Count:	two	8ths	two	8ths	(etc.)

3. Tap and count this rhythm.

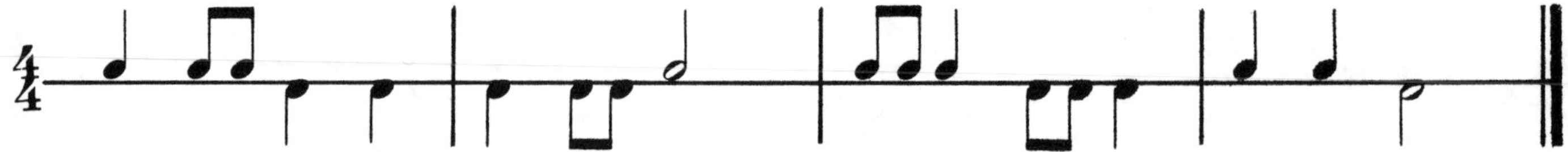

Often four eighth notes are grouped together with a beam: 

4. Tap and count this rhythm.

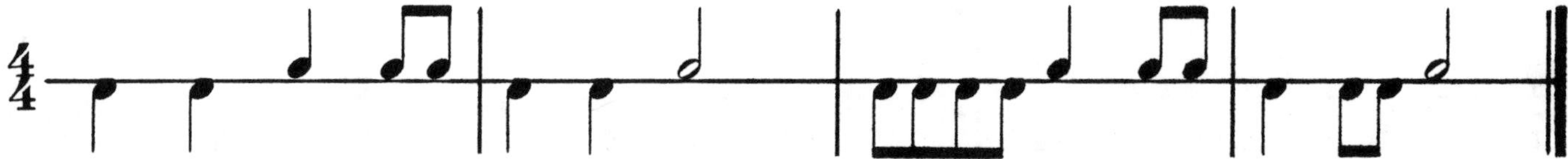

INTERVALS (through the 6th)

Two notes played together form a HARMONIC interval:

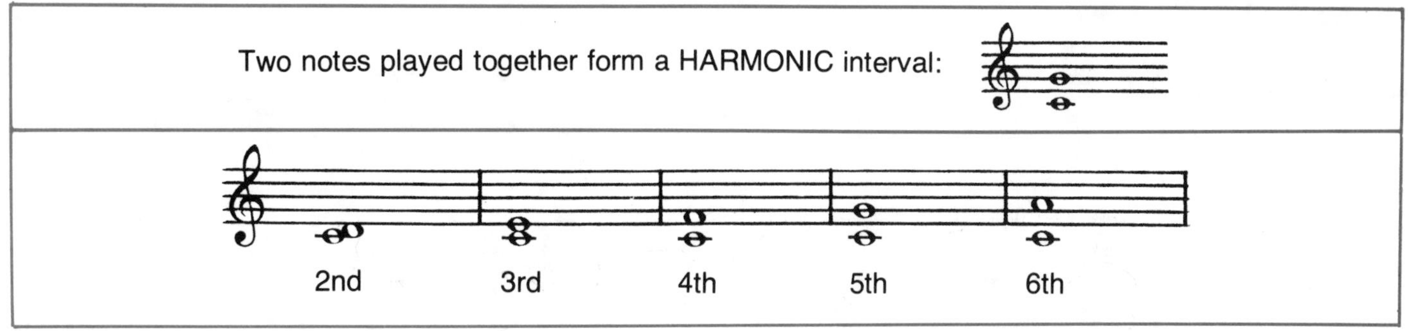

5. Name these harmonic intervals. Play them.

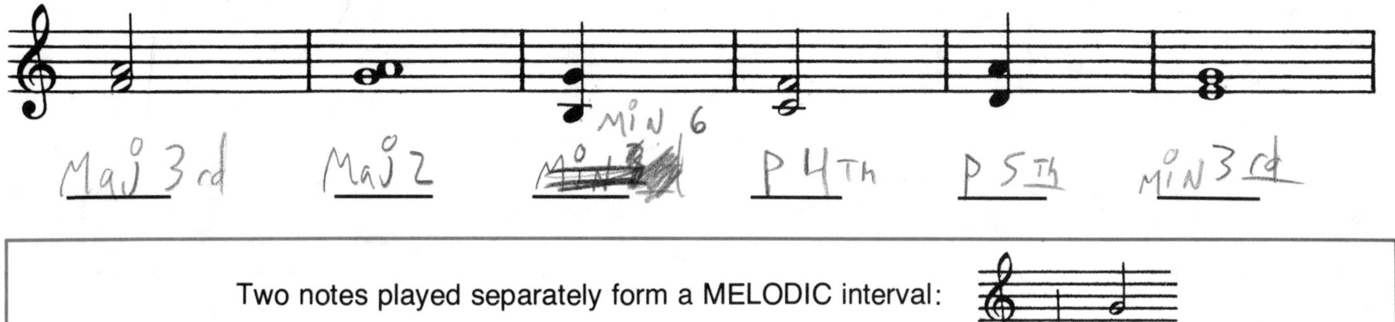

Two notes played separately form a MELODIC interval:

6. Name these melodic intervals. Play them.

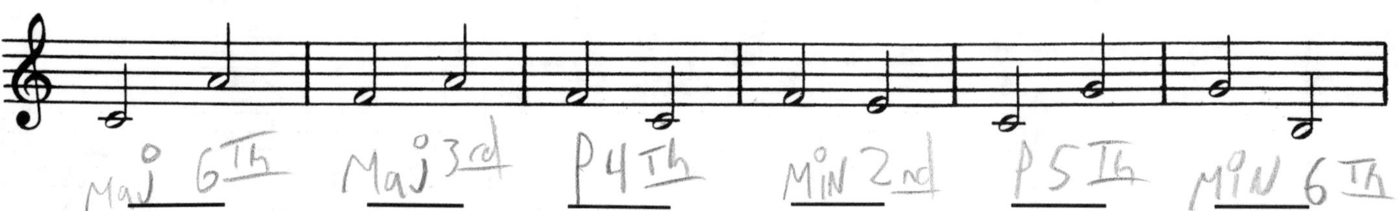

PRIMARY CHORDS IN C MAJOR

The PRIMARY CHORDS of a key are the I, IV, V7 chords. Primary Chords have the following names: I or TONIC chord; IV or SUBDOMINANT chord; V7 or DOMINANT SEVENTH chord. The IV and V7 chords shown are used in relation to the I chord in an easy-to-play arrangement. These IV and V7 chords are arranged in INVERTED position. *

** Chord Symbols

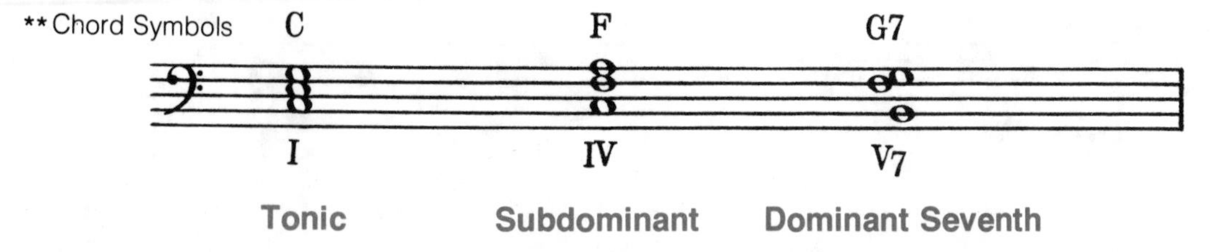

7. Draw the Primary Chords in C Major. Use whole notes. Play these chords.

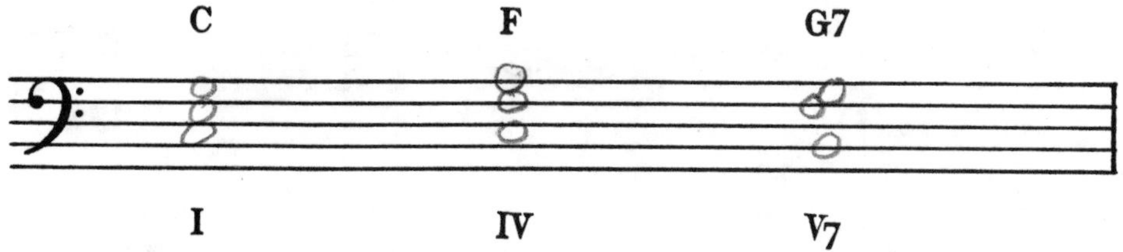

*See page 44 for further explanation of inversions.

**Chord symbols (letter names of chords) are used frequently in popular music. Chord symbols are a form of musical shorthand. Pianists, guitarists, bass players, etc. can improvise accompaniment patterns based on chord symbols.

TECHNIC

5THS - 6THS

Play by "feel." Do not look down at your hands for the stretch of the 6th.

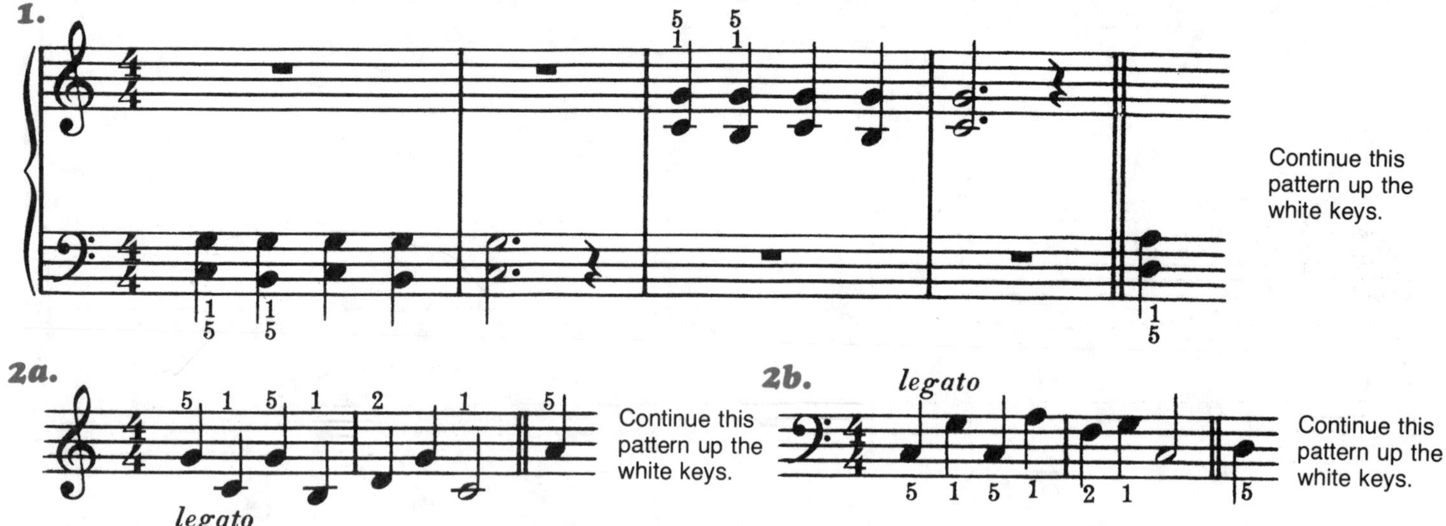

EIGHTH NOTES

Play hands separately at first.

CHORDS

Play by "feel." Do not look down at your hands for the chord changes.

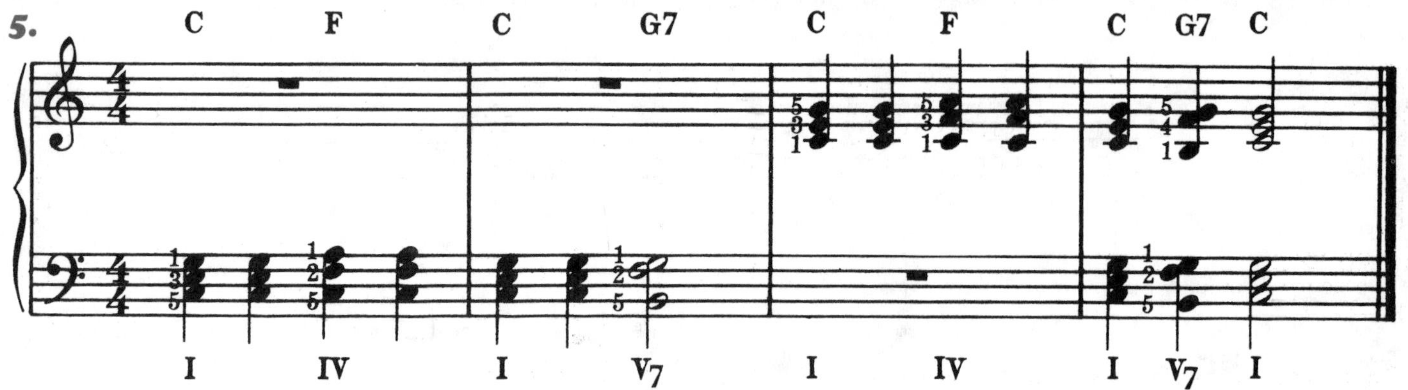

SIGHT READING

PRACTICE DIRECTIONS

Follow the same practice directions given on page 11.*

*Similar practice directions should be followed throughout this book for SIGHT-READING portions.

UNIT 4
THEORY

ACCIDENTALS

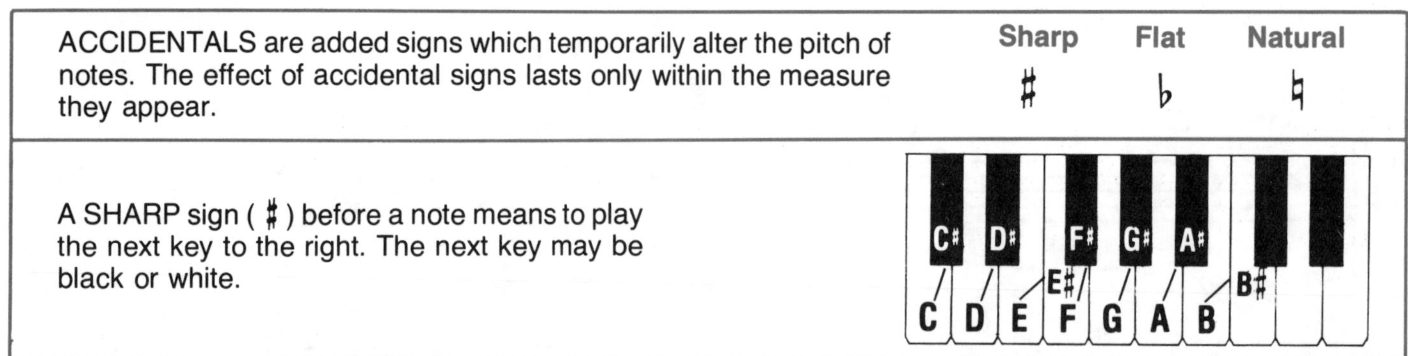

ACCIDENTALS are added signs which temporarily alter the pitch of notes. The effect of accidental signs lasts only within the measure they appear.

A SHARP sign (♯) before a note means to play the next key to the right. The next key may be black or white.

1. Draw a sharp before each note. The "square" in the middle of the sharp is placed on a line or in a space. Say the note names aloud as you play.

A FLAT sign (♭) before a note means to play the next key to the left. The next key may be black or white.

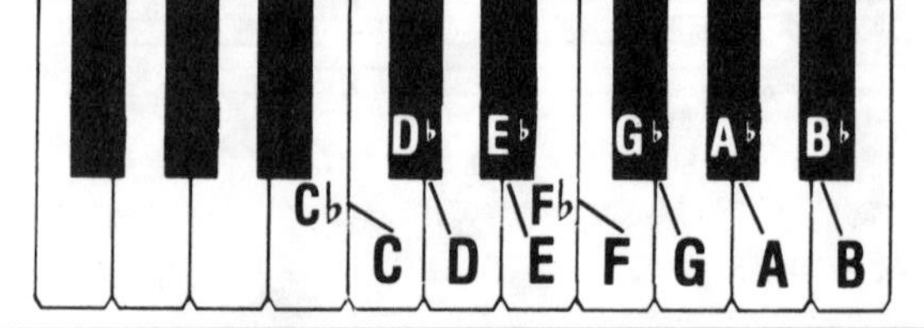

2. Draw a flat before each note. The rounded part of the flat is placed on a line or in a space. Say the note names aloud as you play.

The NATURAL sign (♮) is used to cancel a sharp or flat. It means to play the natural key (white key). Frequently a natural sign is used as a reminder in the next measure.

3. Draw a natural sign before the second note in each measure. The "square" in the middle of the natural is placed on a line or in a space. Play and say these note names aloud.

G MAJOR KEY SIGNATURE

The KEY SIGNATURE consists of the sharps or flats written at the beginning of each staff. (EXCEPTION: the key of C Major has NO sharps or flats.) These sharps or flats are to be played permanently throughout the piece.

SHARP KEY SIGNATURES of Major keys are identified by:

1. naming the last sharp

then, 2. naming the next letter in the musical alphabet (the name of the next note ABOVE the last sharp).

4. Write the G Major key signature after each clef sign.

G MAJOR FIVE FINGER POSITION

The G Major Five Finger Position is G - A - B - C - D.

5. Write the notes for this position in both clefs. Use quarter notes. Play this position.

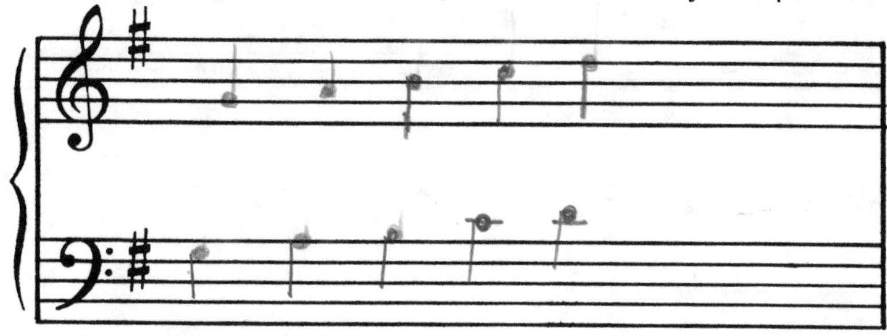

PRIMARY CHORDS IN G MAJOR

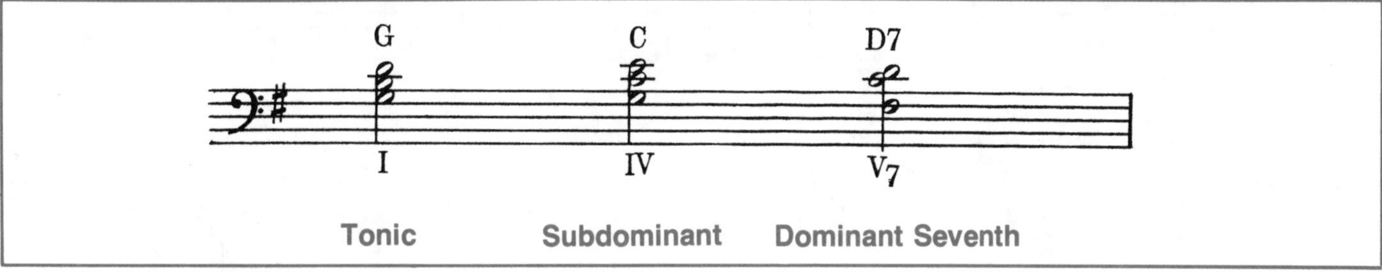

6. Draw the Primary Chords in G Major. Use half notes. Play these chords.

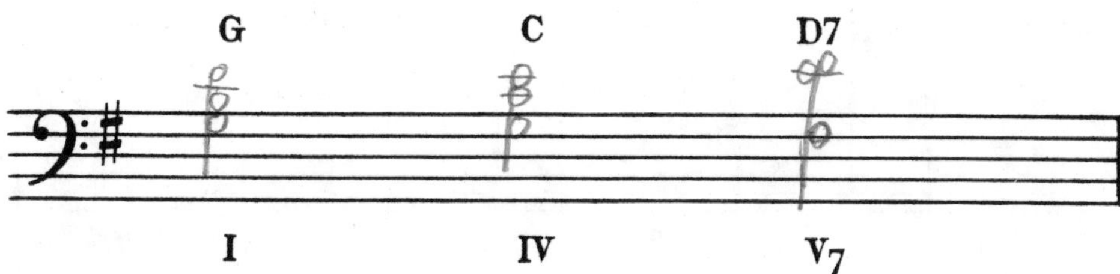

TECHNIC

Play by "feel." Do not look down at your hands for the stretches in the exercises on this page.

5THS - 6THS

1.

EIGHTH NOTES

2a.

2b.

Play hands separately at first.

3.

CHORDS

4.

SIGHT READING

1.

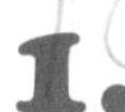

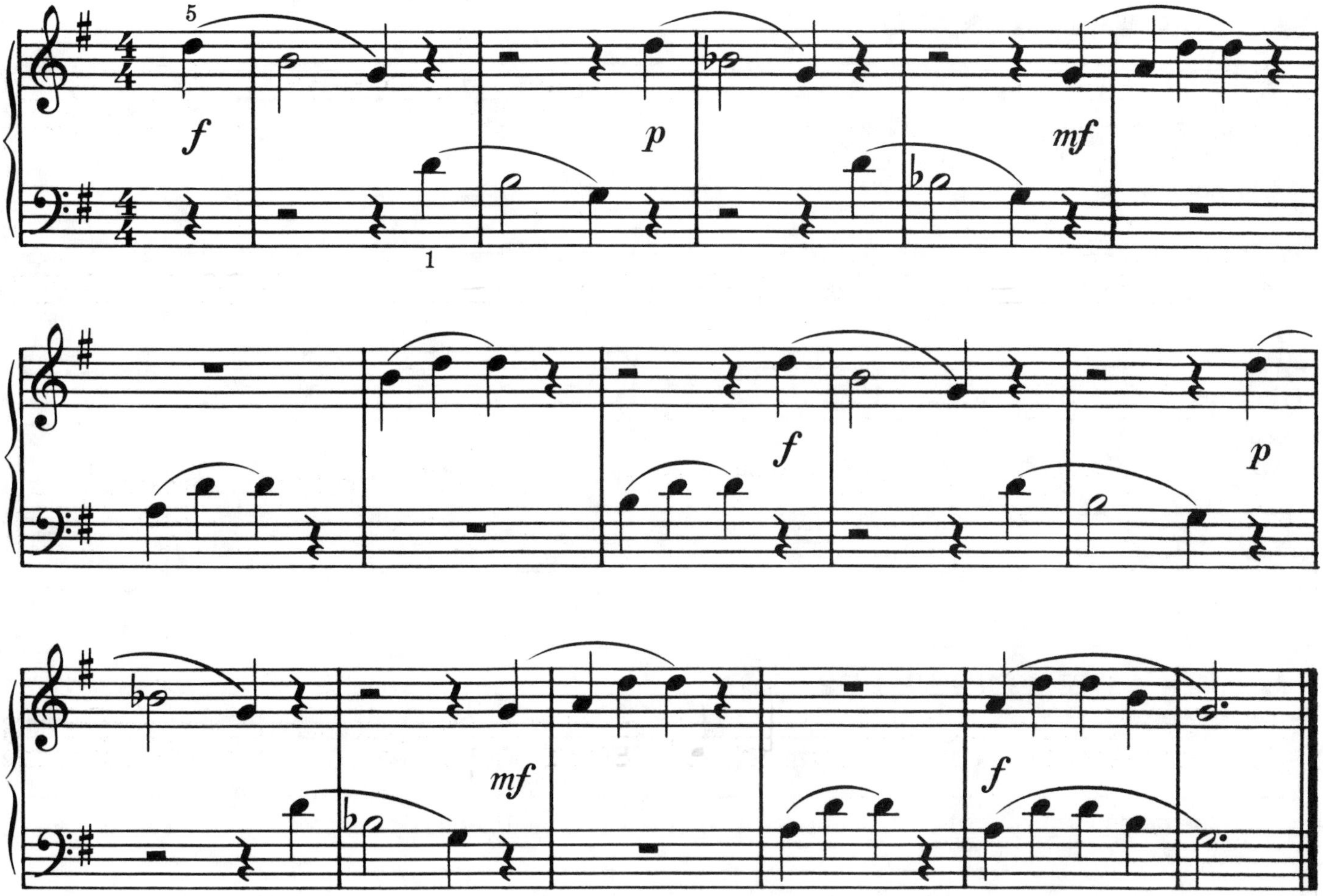

2.

O WORSHIP THE KING
(Hymn)

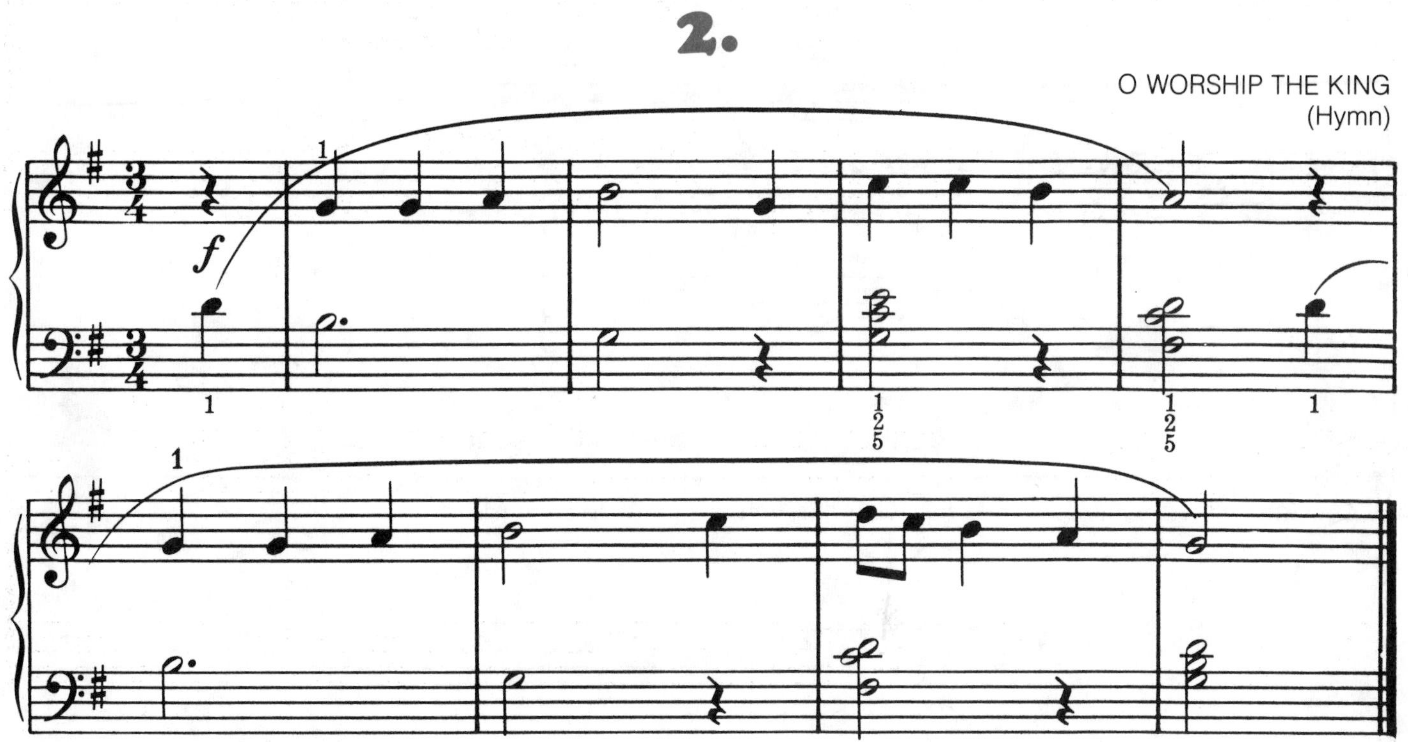

UNIT 5
THEORY

F MAJOR KEY SIGNATURE

The key of F Major has one flat: B-flat. Play all the B's flat in a piece with an F Major key signature.

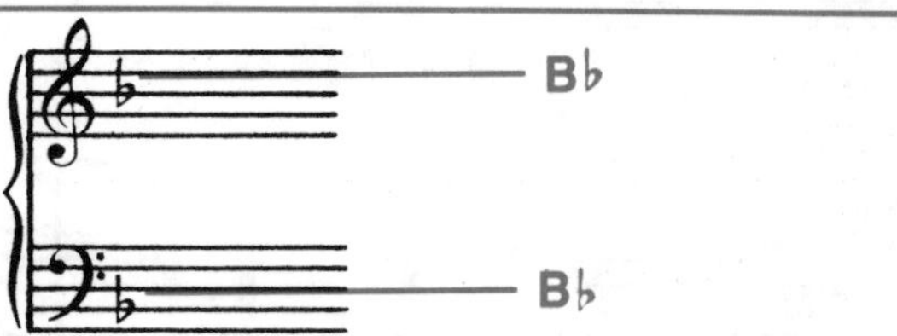

1. Write the F Major key signature after each clef sign.

2. Name the Major key shown by each key signature.

 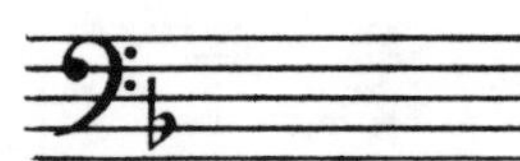  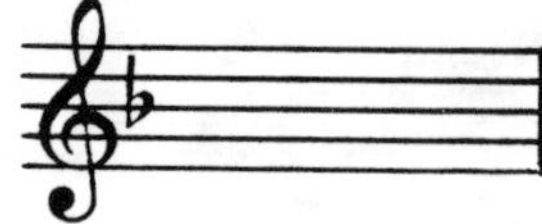

______ ______ ______ ______

F MAJOR FIVE FINGER POSITION

The F Major Five Finger Position is F - G - A - B♭ - C .

3. Write the notes for this position in both clefs. Use quarter notes. Play this position.

PRIMARY CHORDS IN F MAJOR

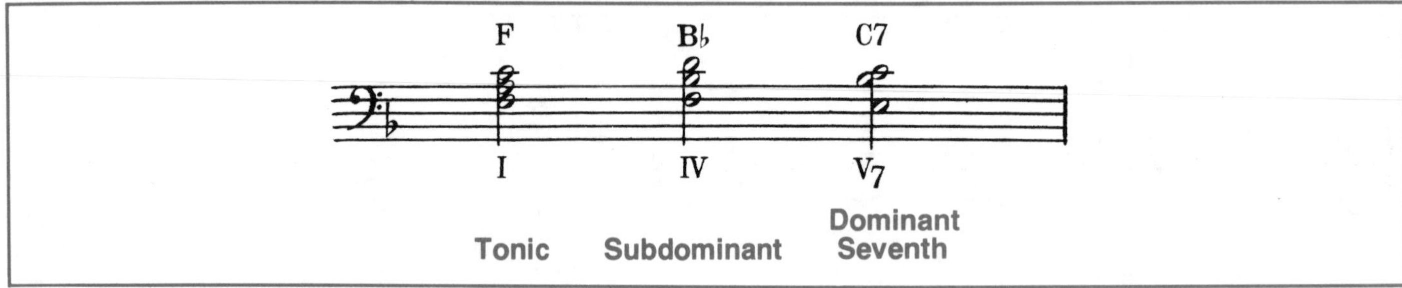

4. Draw the Primary Chords in F Major. Use half notes. Play these chords.

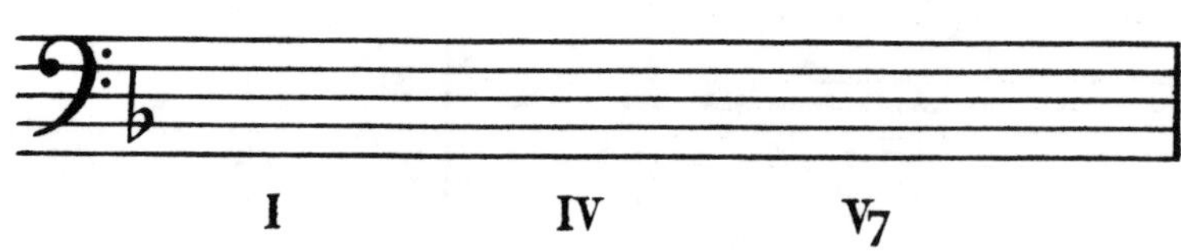

TRANSPOSITION

TRANSPOSITION is the process of writing or playing music in a different key from that in which it was written. The same intervals are used, but transposed to a new key.

5. Draw the notes for this melody transposed to the keys of G and C. Play this melody in all three keys.

DOTTED QUARTER NOTE

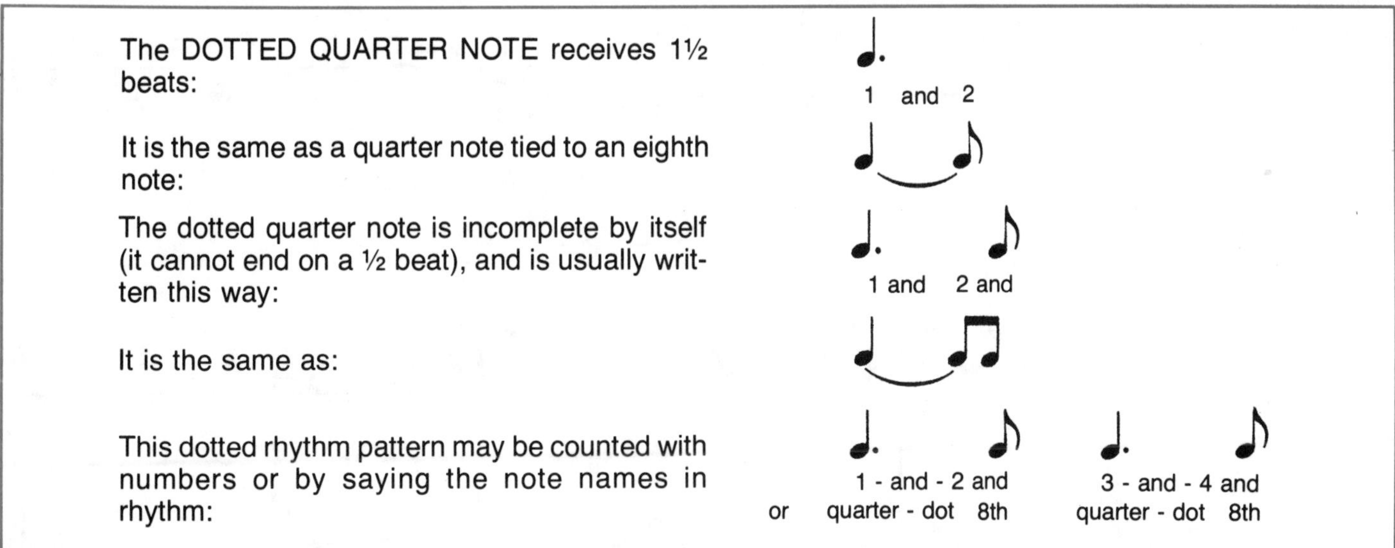

The DOTTED QUARTER NOTE receives 1½ beats:

It is the same as a quarter note tied to an eighth note:

The dotted quarter note is incomplete by itself (it cannot end on a ½ beat), and is usually written this way:

It is the same as:

This dotted rhythm pattern may be counted with numbers or by saying the note names in rhythm:

6. Tap and count this rhythm.

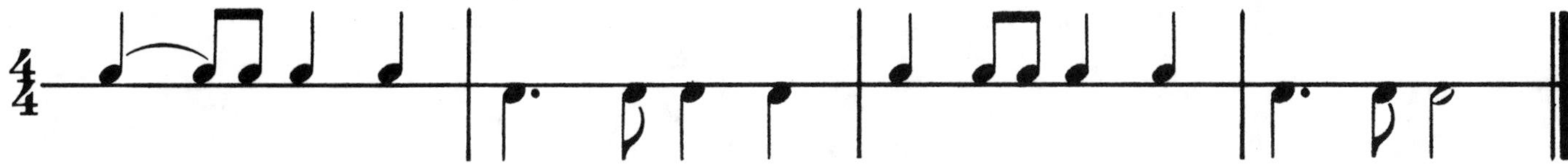

7. Make up (improvise) a melody in the rhythm given. Use notes in the F Major Five Finger Position. Write your melody on this staff.

TECHNIC

Play by "feel." Do not look down at your hands for the stretches in the exercises on this page.

5THS - 6THS

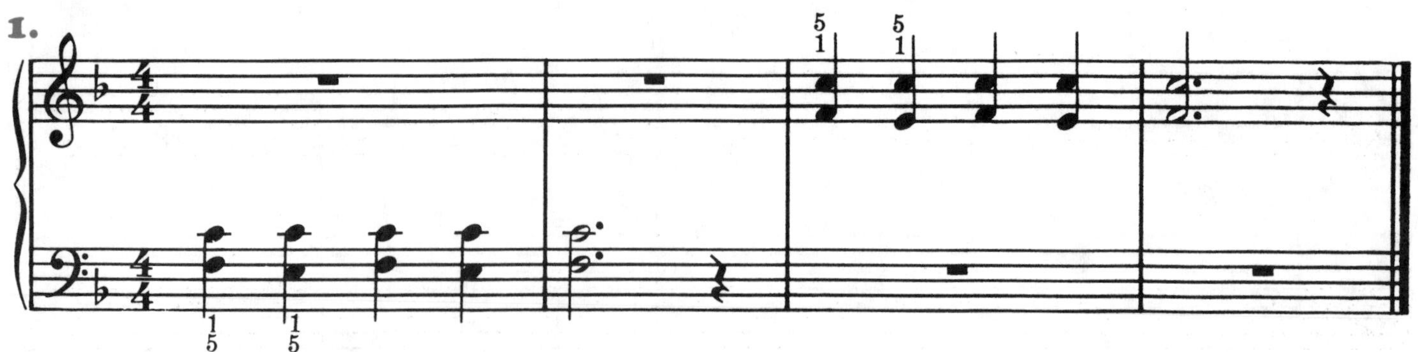

EIGHTH NOTES

Play hands separately at first.

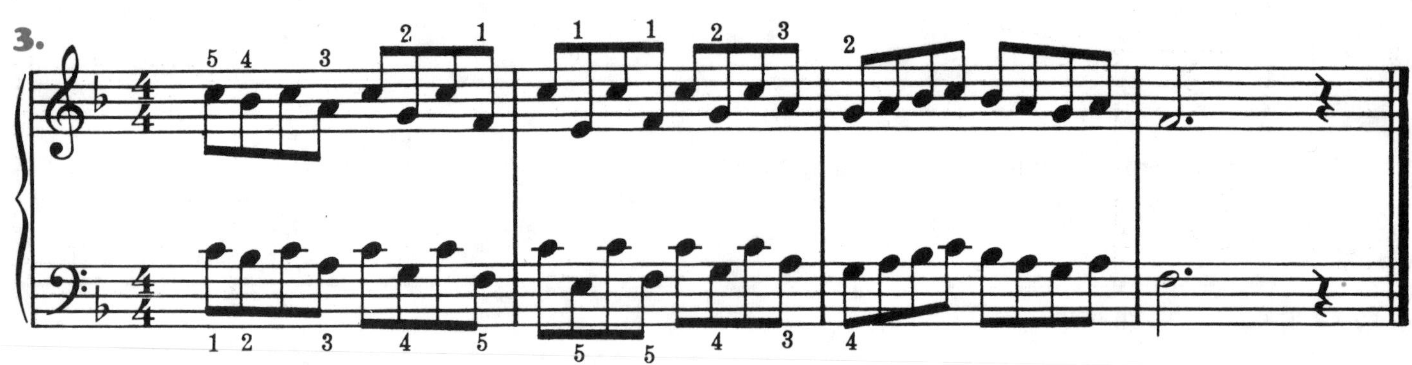

CHORDS

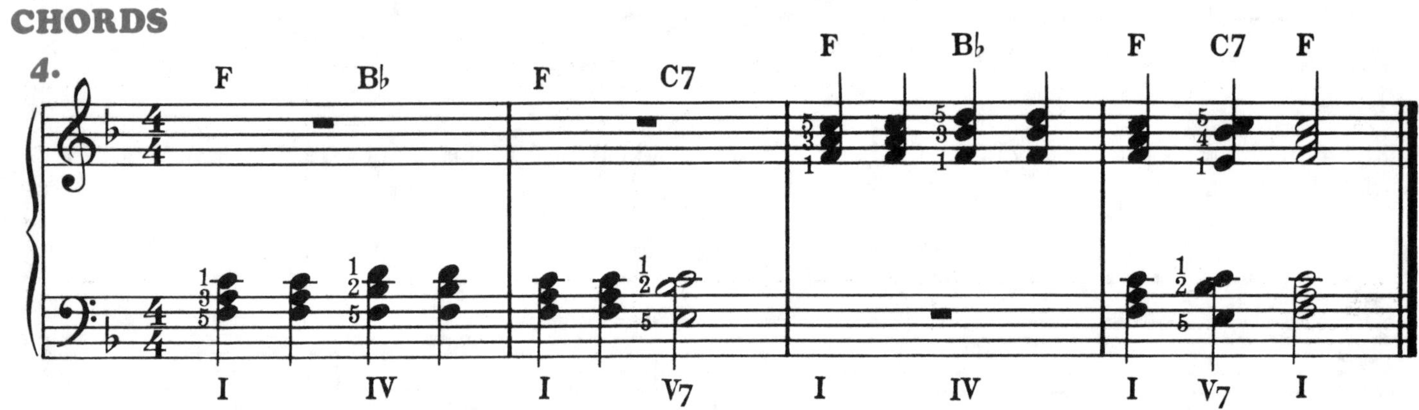

SIGHT READING

UNIT 6
THEORY

THE GROUP 1 KEYS (C, G, F)

The GROUP 1 KEYS are C, G, and F. Each of the I chords is formed with white keys.

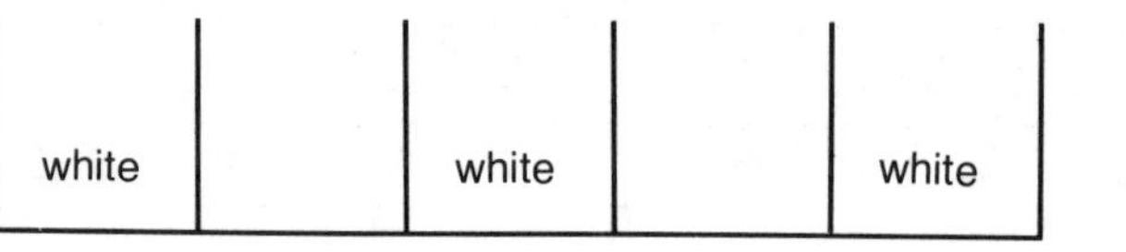

1. Write the I chords in the Group 1 Keys.* Play them.

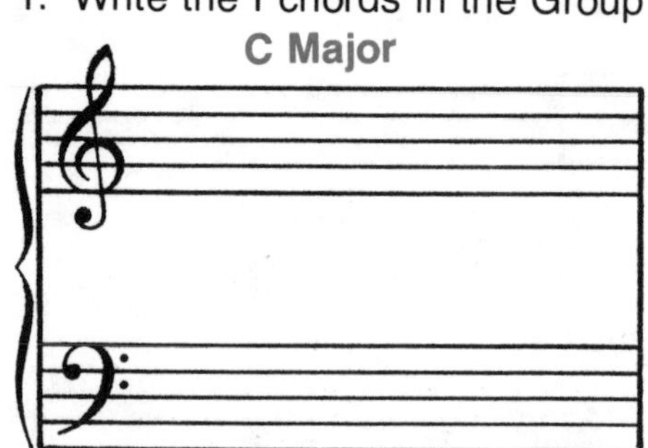

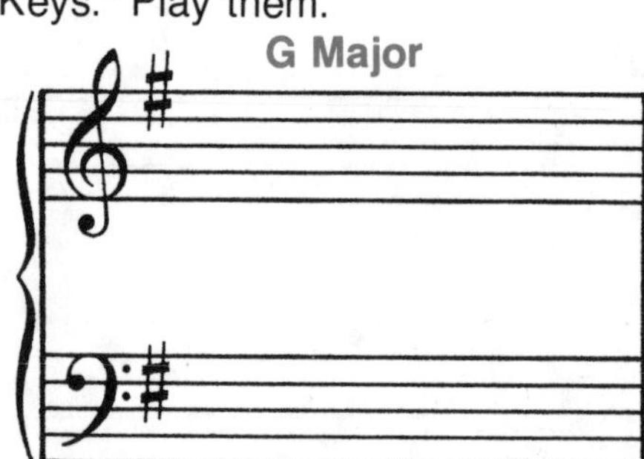

The five finger positions for C and G Major are formed with white keys. F is the unusual key in Group 1, because there is a black key in the five finger position.

2. Write the notes in each five finger position for the Group 1 Keys. Play them.

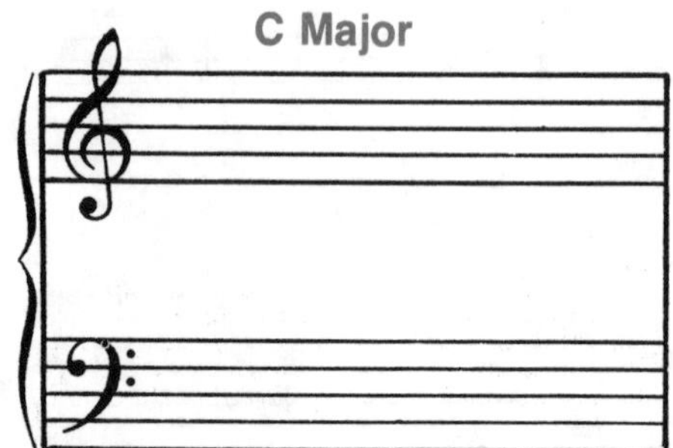

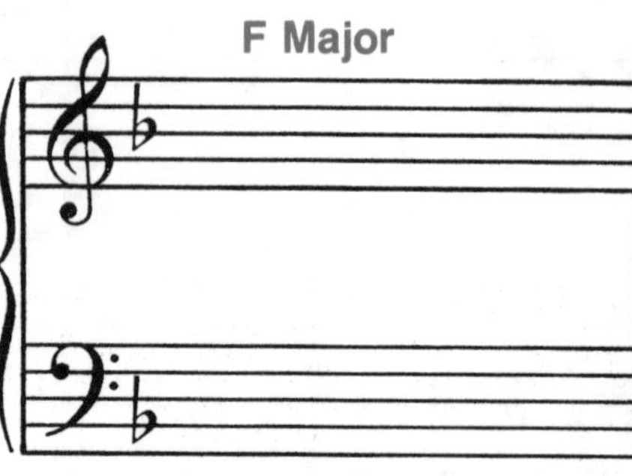

BLOCK AND BROKEN CHORDS

Notes of a chord played at the same time form a BLOCK CHORD:

Notes of a chord played one-at-a-time form a BROKEN CHORD:

3. Write broken chords indicated by the chord symbols.* Play them.

C F G C

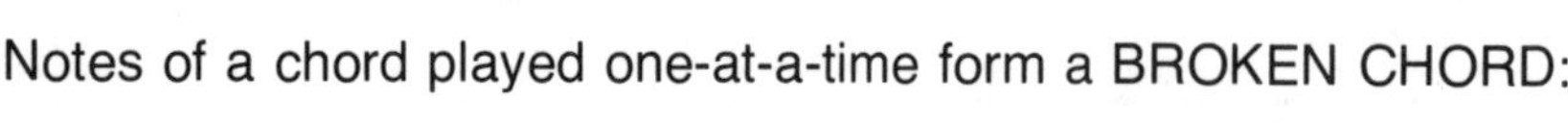

4. Write broken chords indicated by the Roman numerals.** Play them.

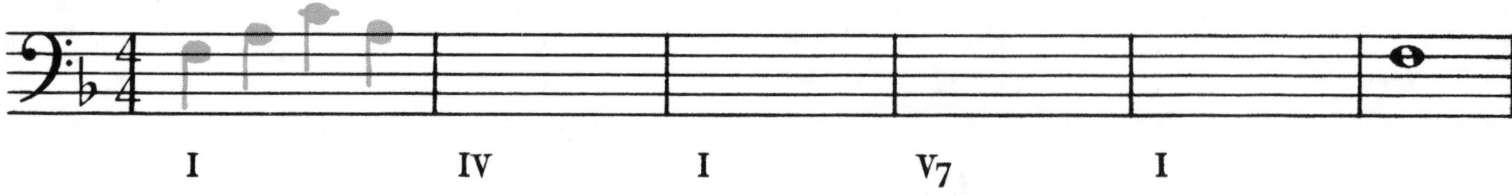

*Teacher: These chords should be written in root position.

**Teacher: The IV and V7 chords should be written in their inverted positions. (See pages 13, 17, and 20.)

STACCATO TOUCH

STACCATO touch is indicated by a dot above or below a note. Staccato means short and disconnected. Staccato is the opposite of legato.

5. Draw dots above or below these notes. The dot goes above or below the note head, opposite the stem. Play these notes staccato.

HARMONIZING MELODIES

6. Write the harmony for these melodies. Write block chords.* Play these pieces.

OLD FOLKS AT HOME

STEPHEN FOSTER

ENGLISH FOLK TUNE

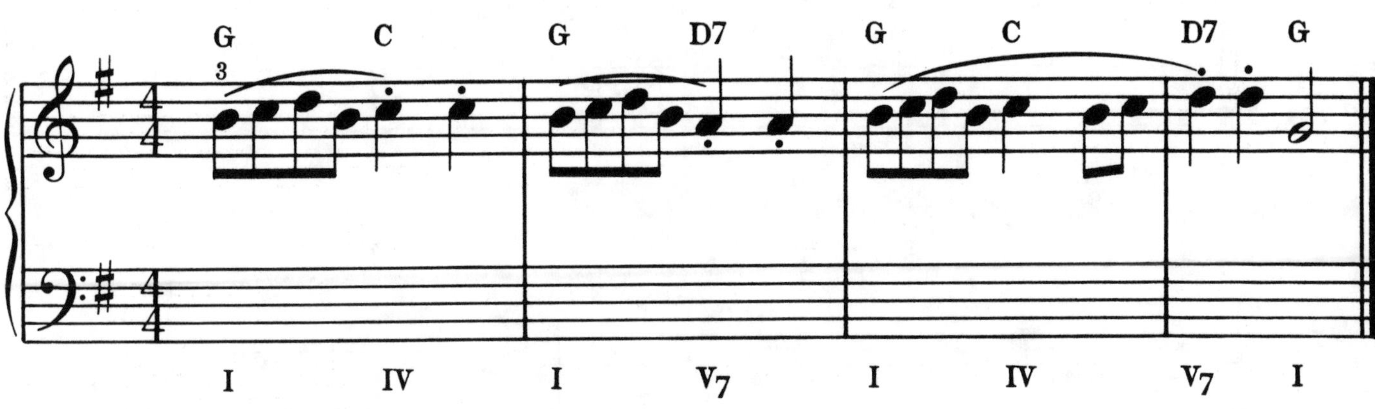

GOOD NIGHT, LADIES

COLLEGE SONG

*Teacher: The IV and V7 chords should be written in their inverted positions.

TECHNIC

STACCATO-LEGATO TOUCH
Transpose the first three exercises on this page to the keys of F and G.
1.
2.
TWO-NOTE SLURS
The wrist should be lower on the first note and higher on the second note in each measure. Say the words "down-up" as you play.
3.
f p
CHANGING HAND POSITIONS
1st time - LEGATO
2nd time - STACCATO
4.

SIGHT READING

UNIT 7
THEORY

HALF STEPS AND WHOLE STEPS

From one key to the nearest key with no key in between is a HALF STEP.

From one key to a neighbor key with one key in between is a WHOLE STEP.

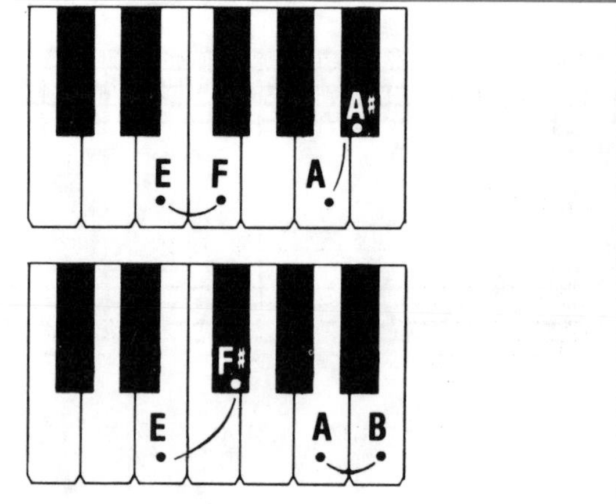

1. Write 1/2 for half step and 1 for whole step. Play these half and whole steps.

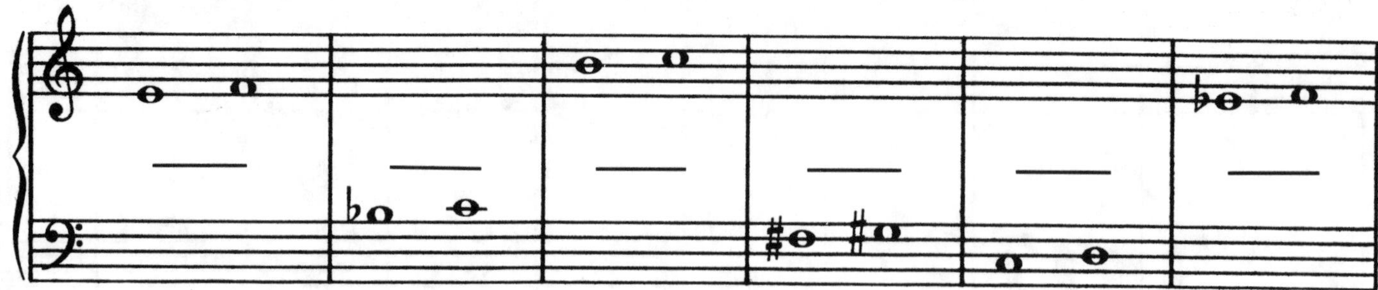

FORMATION OF MAJOR SCALES

There are eight tones in the Major scale. The tones are called SCALE DEGREES. The scale degrees are arranged in a pattern of whole steps and half steps. The first note in the scale is called the keynote.

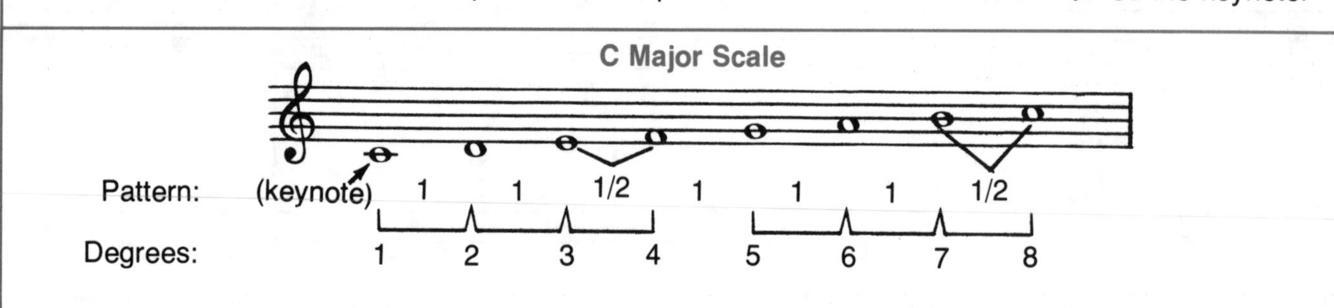

2. Draw the notes of the C Major scale using whole notes. Mark the half steps with a V . Write 1 for whole step and 1/2 for half step. Write in the fingering.* Play this scale first with your Right Hand, then with your Left Hand.

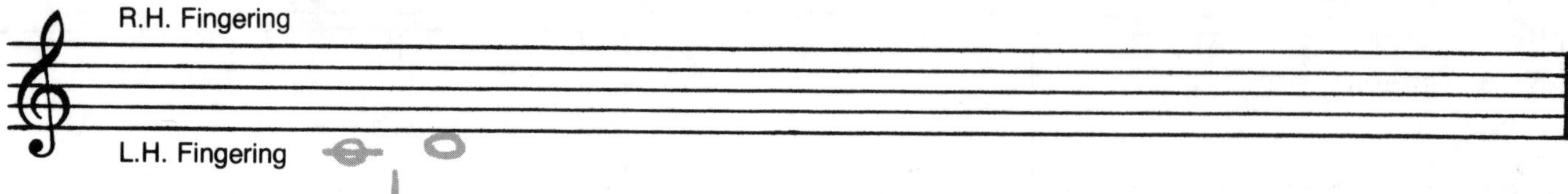

*See page 45 for the C Major scale fingering.

QUESTION AND ANSWER PHRASES

A musical phrase is a musical sentence. Phrases follow each other in music like sentences in a paragraph. One phrase may ask a "question." The question phrase will end on a note OTHER than the keynote. Another phrase may give an "answer." The answer phrase will end ON the keynote.

3. Play these examples of question and answer phrases. Notice that the question phrase is the same in both examples.

Examples:

4. Below are some two-measure question phrases. Make up (improvise) two-measure answer phrases to complete these lines. Write your best "answers" on the staffs. Use the rhythm of the question in your answer. Use notes in the five finger pattern of the key for your answer.

Key of C Major

Key of F Major

Key of G Major

TECHNIC

C MAJOR SCALE STUDIES

Practice these studies turning the thumb under or crossing over the thumb as smoothly as possible.

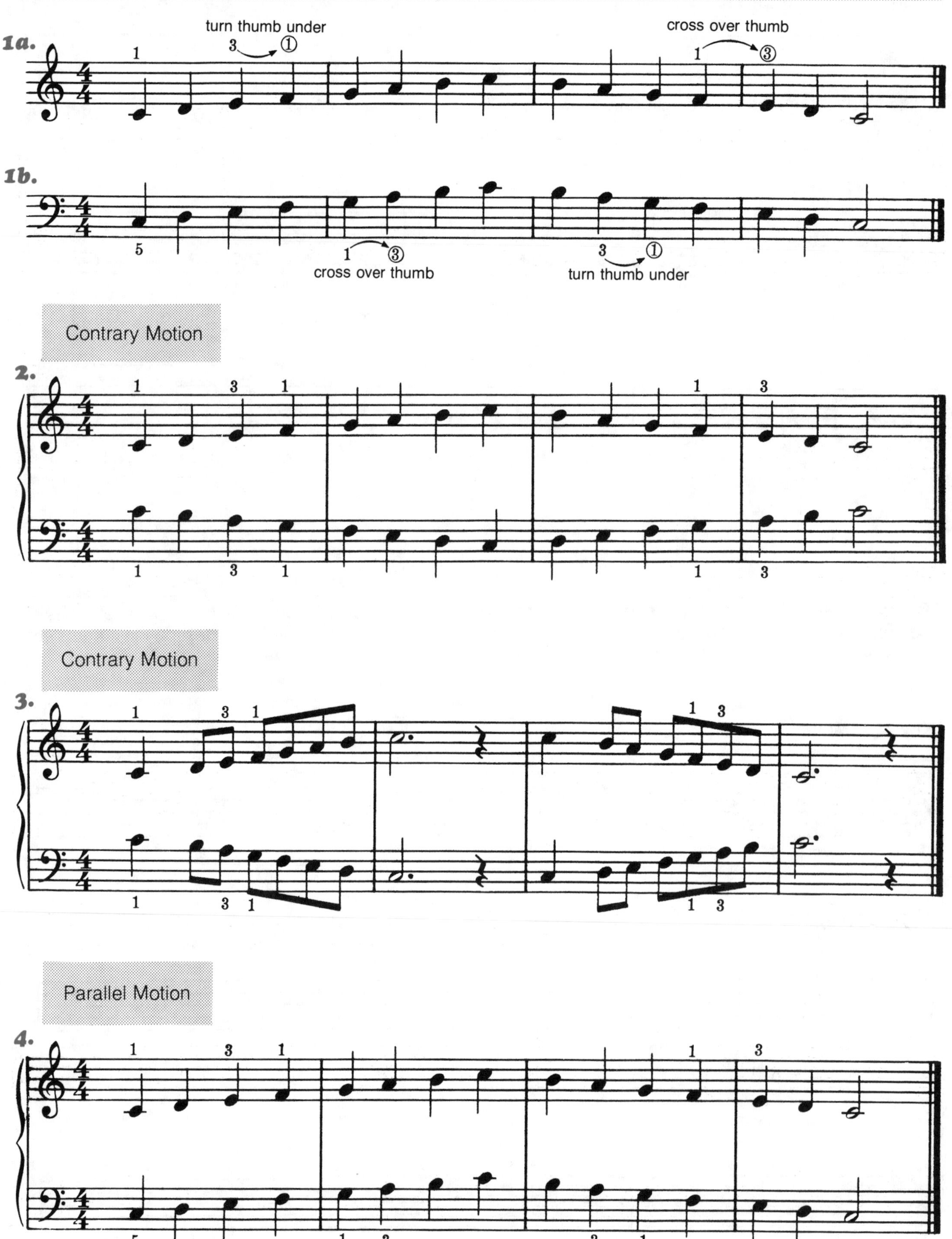

SIGHT READING

UNIT 8
THEORY

G MAJOR SCALE

1. Draw the notes of the G Major scale using whole notes. Mark the half steps with a V . Write in the fingering.* Play this scale first with your Right Hand, then with your Left Hand.

R.H. Fingering

L.H. Fingering

$\frac{6}{8}$ TIME SIGNATURE

All time signatures have two numbers. The upper number tells how many beats there are in a measure. The lower number tells the kind of note that gets one beat.

6 – 6 beats to the measure

8 – an eighth note (♪) gets one beat

Time Values in $\frac{6}{8}$

Notes		Rests	
♪	1 beat	𝄾	1 beat
♩	2 beats	𝄽	2 beats
♩.	3 beats	𝄽.	3 beats
𝅗𝅥.	6 beats	𝄽. 𝄽. (𝄼)	6 beats

2. Tap and count this rhythm.

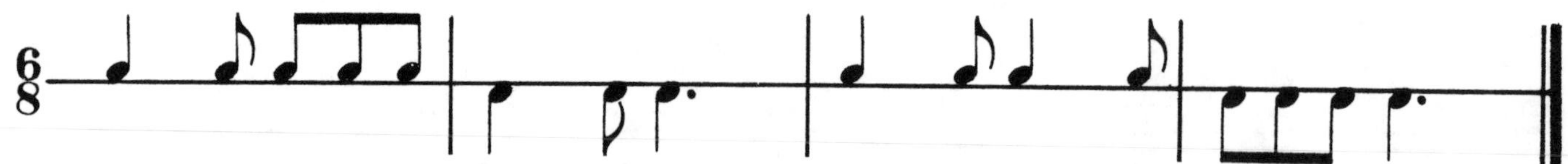

3. Make up (improvise) a melody in the rhythm given. Use notes in the G Major scale. Write your melody on this staff.

*See page 45 for the G Major scale fingering.

QUESTION AND ANSWER PHRASES

4. Make up (improvise) two-measure answer phrases to complete these lines. Write your best "answers" on the staffs.

HARMONIZING LEAD LINES

A LEAD LINE is the written melody of a song. No bass part is given. The pianist must improvise (make up) a bass part. The CHORD SYMBOLS (shown above the melody) tell which chords to use in the bass.	To read the chord symbols, remember this: C = I chord in C F = IV chord in C G = V7 chord in C

5. Play ***AMERICA***, harmonizing (playing chords) with your Left Hand. Always play a Left Hand chord on the first beat of each measure. If no chord symbol is given in the next measure, repeat the same chord from the measure before.

AMERICA

TECHNIC

PHRASING STUDY (6/8 Rhythm)

Transpose: F, C

G MAJOR SCALE STUDIES

Transpose: C

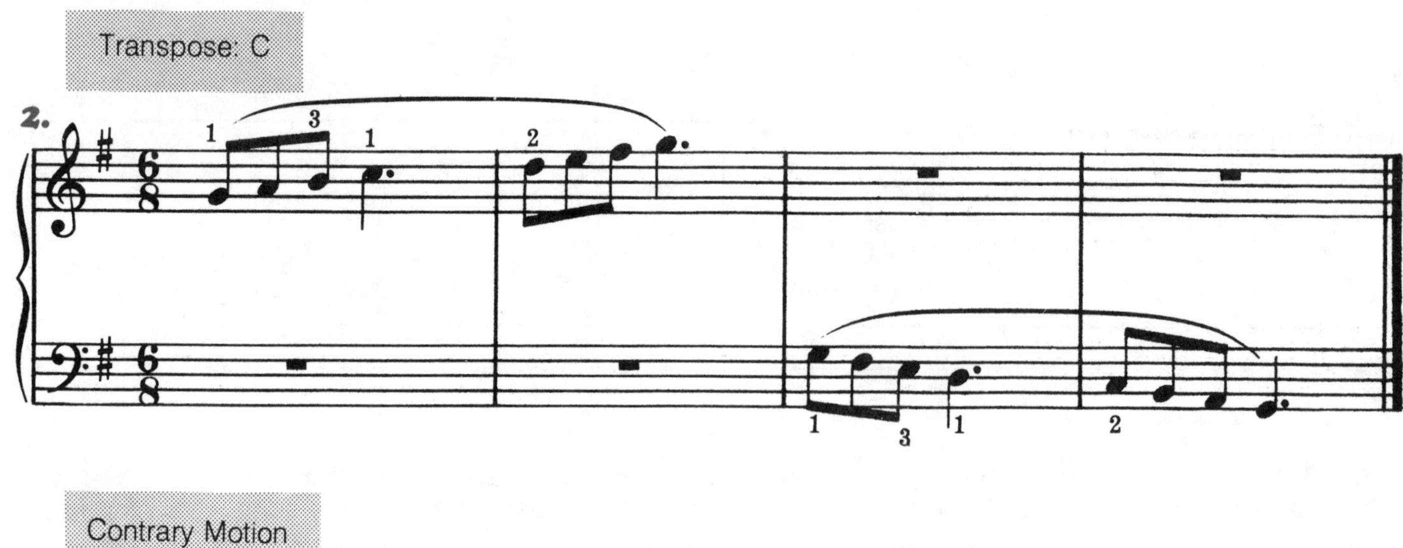

Contrary Motion

Parallel Motion

SIGHT READING

UNIT 9
THEORY

F MAJOR SCALE

1. Draw the notes of the F Major scale. Mark the half steps with a V. Write in the fingering.* Play this scale first with your Right Hand, then with your Left Hand.

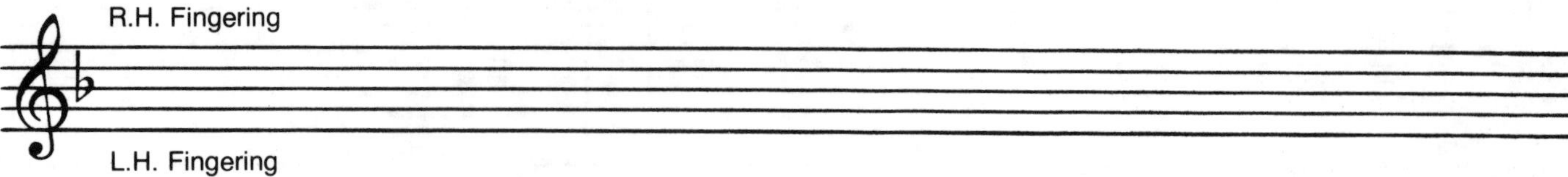

INTERVALS (through the Octave)

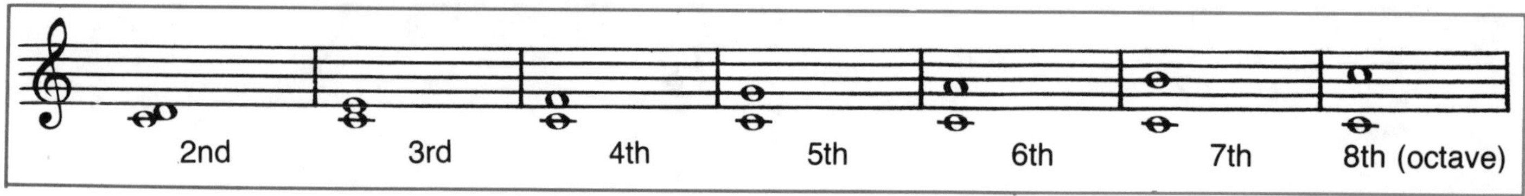

2. Name these harmonic intervals. Play them.

3. Name these melodic intervals. Play them.

THE ORDER OF SHARPS

The SHARPS are ALWAYS written in this order on the staff.

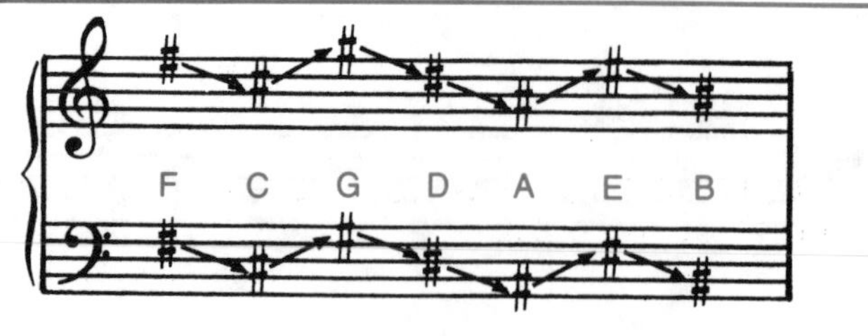

4. Write the order of sharps three times on this staff.

*See page 45 for the F Major scale fingering.

MAJOR SHARP KEY SIGNATURES

To find the Major key name of a piece with sharps in the key signature:

1. name the LAST sharp to the right then,
2. name the next letter in the musical alphabet (go up a half step).

   This is the name of the Major key.

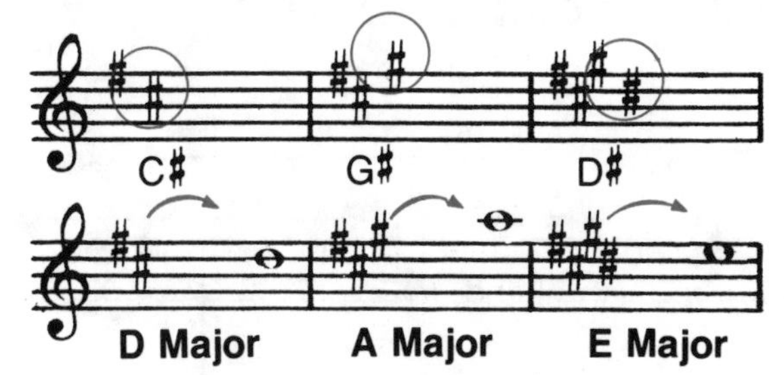

5. Name these Major key signatures.

THE GROUP 2 KEYS (D, A, E)

The GROUP 2 KEYS are D, A, and E. Each of the I chords is formed with a pattern of "white - black - white" keys.

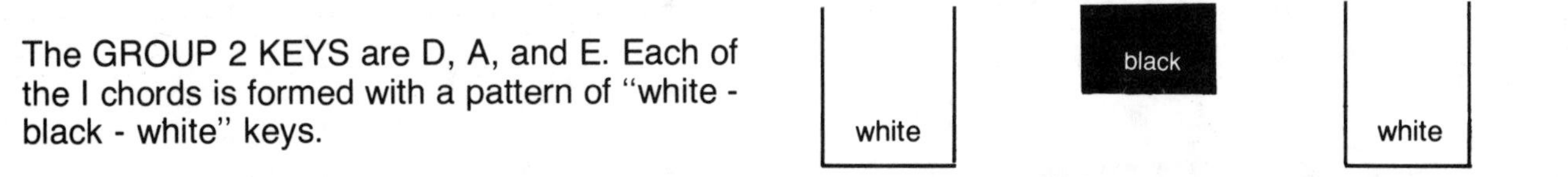

6. Write the I chords in the Group 2 Keys. Add the necessary sharps. Play these chords.

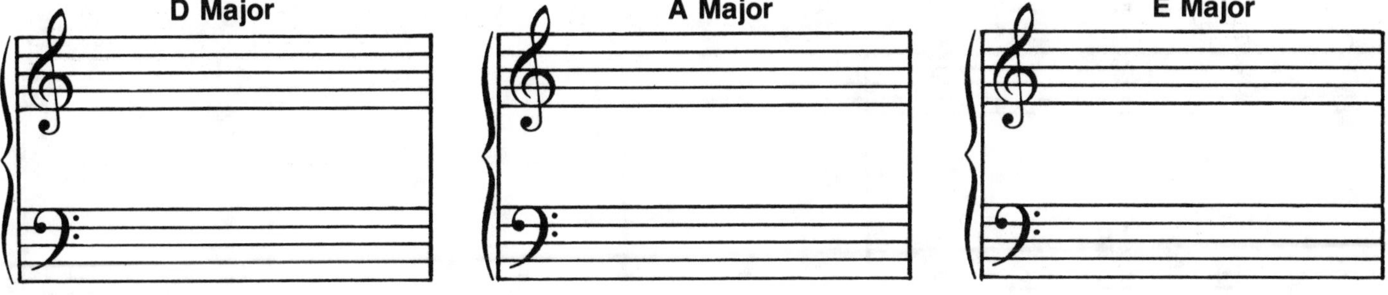

The five finger positions for D and A have only one black key. E is the unusual key in Group 2, because there are two black keys in the five finger position.

7. Write the notes in each five finger position for the Group 2 Keys. Add the necessary sharps. Play these positions.

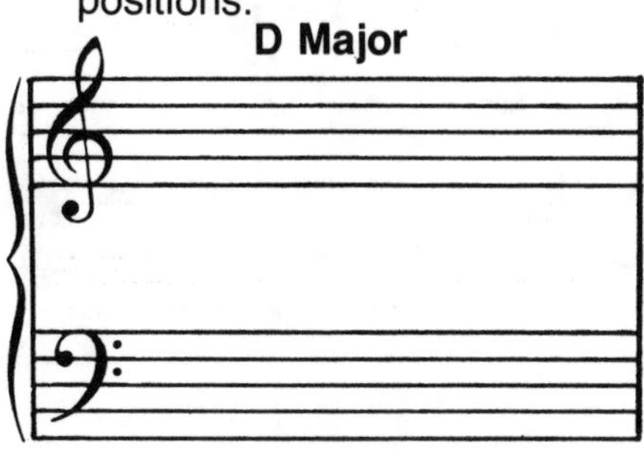

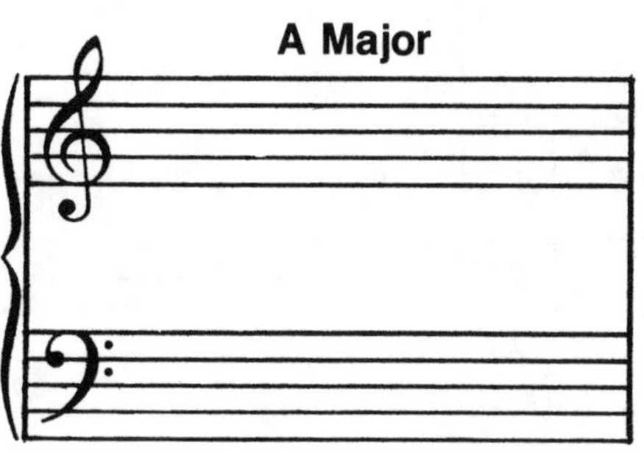

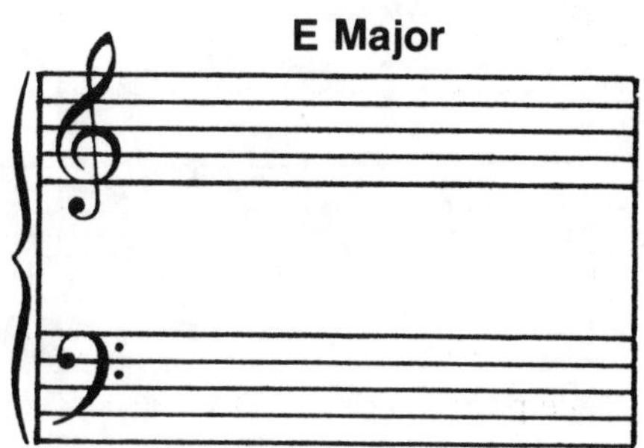

TECHNIC

F MAJOR SCALE STUDIES

Transpose: G, C

GROUP 2 CHORD STUDIES *

Transpose: A, E

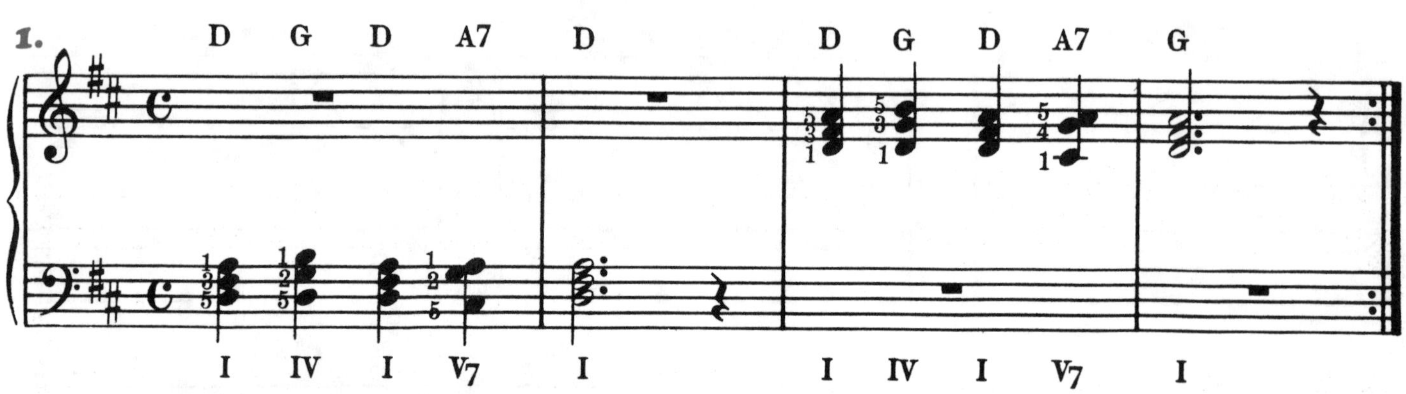

Transpose: A, E   Practice hands separately at first.

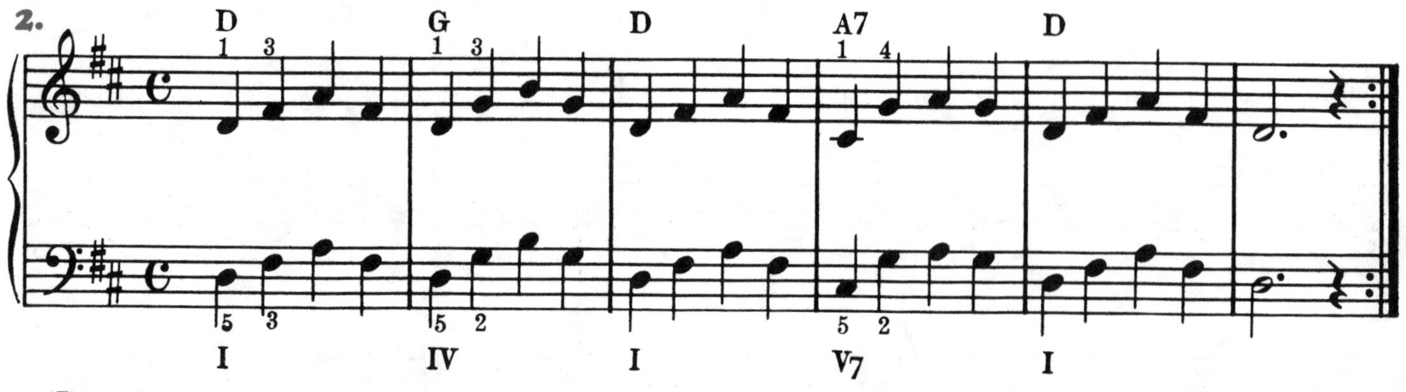

*The scales of D, A, and E are written on page 45.

SIGHT READING

UNIT 10
THEORY

MINOR CHORDS

To write a minor chord, LOWER the MIDDLE NOTE of a Major chord ONE HALF STEP.

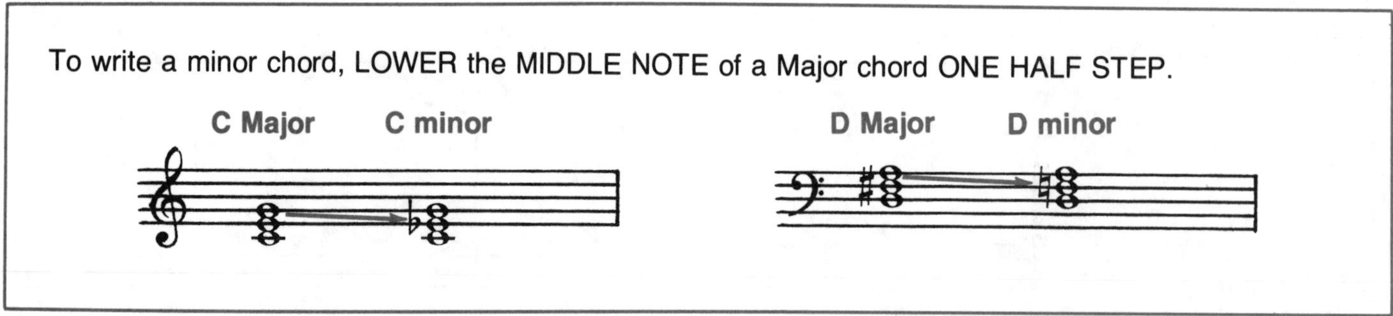

1. After each Major chord, write a minor chord. When you lower the middle note, DO NOT change the letter name. Lower a natural to a FLAT. Lower a sharp to a NATURAL. Play these chords.

GROUP 1 KEYS

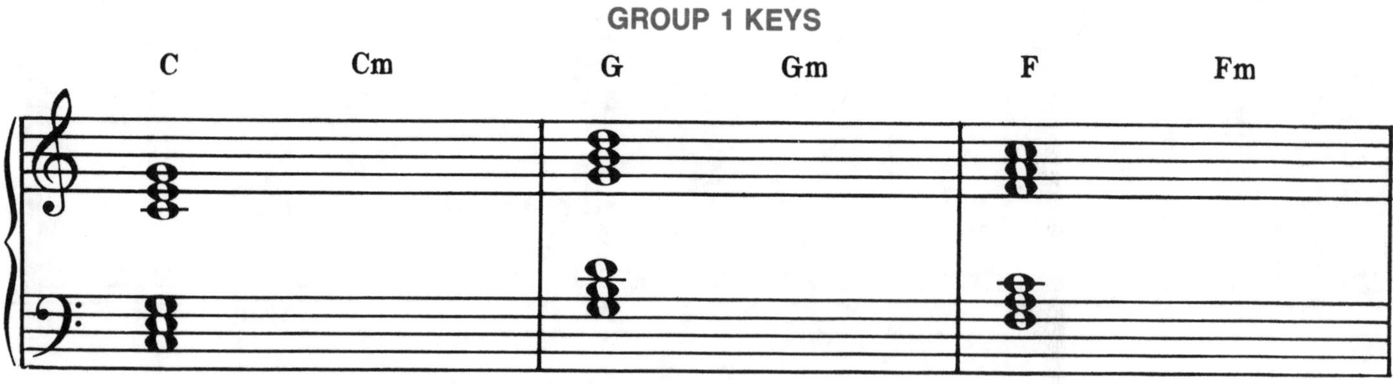

GROUP 2 KEYS

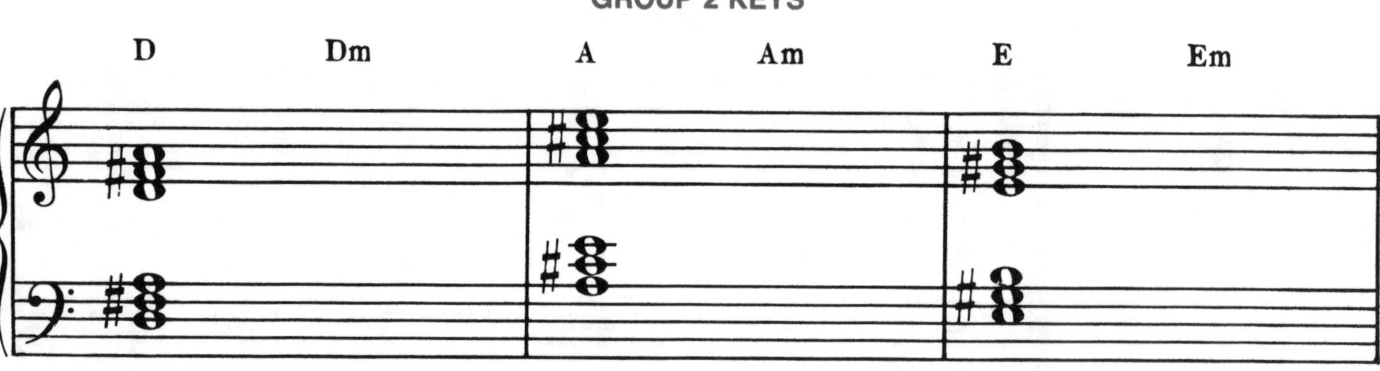

2. Name and play these Major and minor chords.

QUESTION AND ANSWER PHRASES

3. Make up (improvise) two-measure answer phrases to complete these lines. Write your best "answers" on the staffs.

HARMONIZING LEAD LINES

To read the chord symbols, remember this:
G= I chord in G
C= IV chord in G
D7= V7 chord in G

4. Play ***SHE'LL BE COMIN' ROUND THE MOUNTAIN***, harmonizing (playing chords) with your Left Hand. Always play a Left Hand chord on the first beat of each measure.* If no chord symbol is given in the next measure, repeat the same chord from the measure before.

SHE'LL BE COMIN' ROUND THE MOUNTAIN

Teacher: the melody may be played one octave higher to avoid right and left hand conflicts.

TECHNIC

MAJOR - MINOR CHORDS

1.

2.

SIGHT READING

REFERENCE

EXPLANATION OF PRIMARY CHORDS

All chords are built on scale degrees. The Primary Chords are built on the 1st, 4th, and 5th degrees of the scale.

The I and IV chords are three-note chords (triads). These chords have a root and the intervals of a 3rd and 5th.

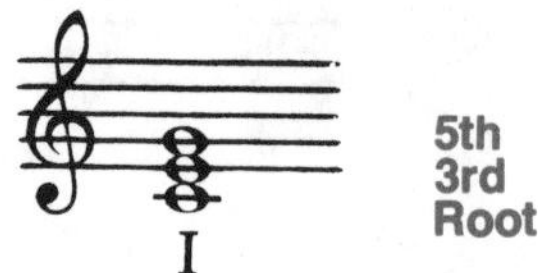

Every chord may be inverted (rearranged) by moving the position of the root.

You have played the IV chord in inverted position (second inversion) in an easy-to-play arrangement.

You have played the V7 chord, rather than the V chord, for a fuller sound. The V7 chord has a root and the intervals of a 3rd, 5th, and 7th.

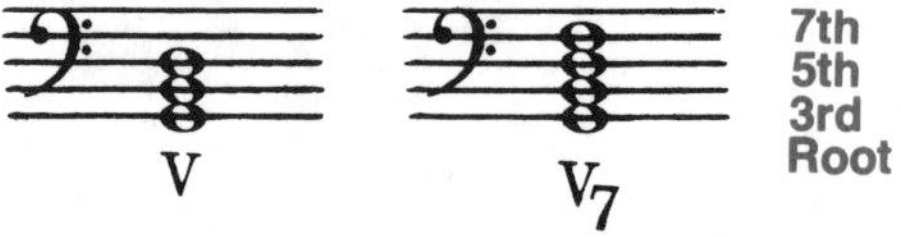

You have played the V7 chord in its first inversion with the 5th omitted.

The arrangement of the Primary Chords you have played consists of the I chord in Root Position, the IV chord in Second Inversion, and the V7 chord in First Inversion with the 5th omitted.

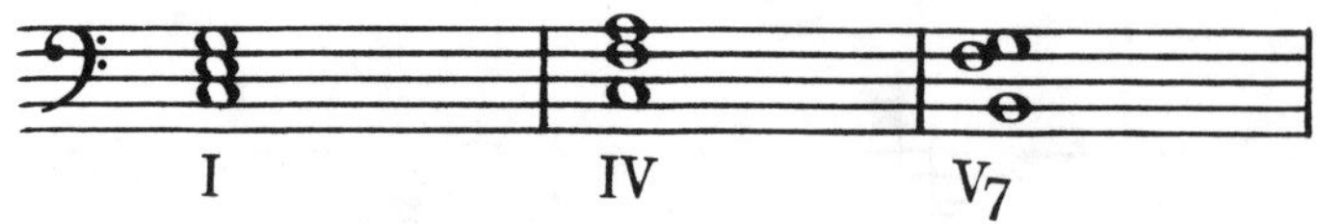

MAJOR SCALES AND PRIMARY CHORDS

(GROUP 1 AND 2 KEYS)

MANUSCRIPT PAPER

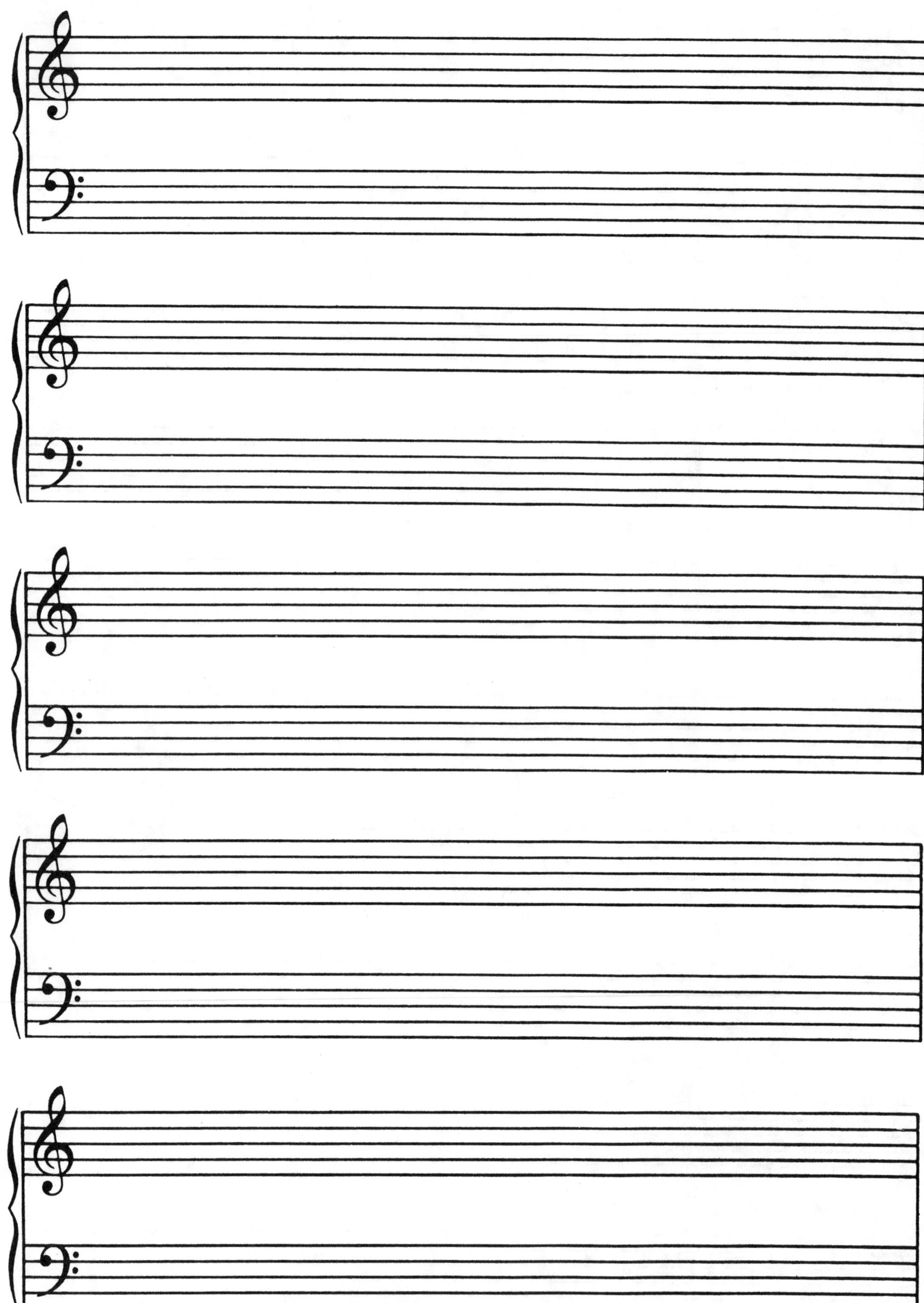